Teaching Ideas That Make Learning Fun

TEACHING IDEAS THAT
MAKE LEARNING
FUN

Matilda J. Peck

Corrective Reading Teacher
Bridgewater-Raritan (N.J.)
Regional School District

Morton J. Schultz

Technical Communications Consultant

PARKER PUBLISHING COMPANY, INC.
West Nyack, N.Y.

© 1969 BY

PARKER PUBLISHING COMPANY, INC.
WEST NYACK, N.Y.

LIBRARY OF CONGRESS
CATALOG CARD NUMBER: 69-17071

PRINTED IN THE UNITED STATES OF AMERICA
B & P

HOW TO USE THIS BOOK
FOR MAXIMUM ADVANTAGE

No idea is so antiquated that it was not once modern. The art of teaching is the art of assisting discovery.

These thoughts permit an understanding of why books of this nature are important.

As an elementary school teacher, you have certain tools besides your knowledge with which to work—your voice and personality, and various mechanical aids.

There are, however, certain forces present in every classroom that interfere with teaching. For instance, every student is a different personality. Some are slow—some are bright. Some have personal problems. Others are very stable.

The teacher is often in a constant struggle with the negative forces. Many times the tools she has at her disposal are not enough, and she needs something that will bring the attention of every student to the thought, concept, or bit of knowledge she is trying to teach. That "something" is often an idea.

This book is a compendium of such ideas. The purpose of each is to allow you to better utilize the tools you already have, to permit formation of a common bond between you and your students, and to enhance student attention.

You will find some ideas in this book with which you are familiar. You may be using some. Others will be new to you. Whatever the case, each has been included for its ability to accomplish one of the objectives cited above.

In using this book, keep in mind that the authors do not intend it to be read and then put aside. Instead, it is intended as a *reference* to keep before you in planning your day-to-day lessons. If you need a novel way of presenting a science or reading concept, for example, turn to the chapter on science or reading.

Also keep in mind that usually only one or two ideas per lesson are needed to evoke student interest. One game after another thrown at a class will hamper the learning process. Use the ideas judiciously.

Matilda J. Peck and Morton J. Schultz

CONTENTS

6. IDEAS TO USE IN DEVELOPING LISTENING ABILITY 85

Ways to Evaluate Development of Listen .g Ability · Developing the Ability to Listen · Learning to Listen Through Self-Evaluation · Fostering Observation and Sequence Skills · Training the Ear · The Use of Reading to Enhance Listening · Auditory Discrimination of Sounds · Following Directions

7. IDEAS TO USE IN TEACHING SOCIAL STUDIES . 93

Summary of Activities · Classroom TV · Politics in the Classroom · Learning About Community Helpers · How to Make "Helpers" Come Alive · Flag Waving · A Room Full of Indians · Pottery Making · Jigsaw Puzzles · Tom-Tom · Map Ideas · Getting to Know the Community · Overhead Projection for Map Studies · Talks by Local Officials · Another Community Idea · Meeting the Post Office · Getting the Most from a Social Studies Unit on Communication · Sports and Geography · Making Booklets · Matching Up Matchsticks · Social Study Unit Considerations for Lower Grades · Planning Unit Sequences · Ideas to Use for a Transportation Unit · Use of the Sandtable in the Social Studies Program · Additional Ideas with the Overhead Projector

8. TEACHING ARITHMETIC THROUGH ACTIVITY . 117

Let's Go Fishing · A Card Game for Small Groups · The Spinning Wheel · You're It · Ring-Toss Game · Number Aids · Tic-Tac-Toe, Arithmetic Style · More Tic-Tac-Toe · Young Person's Bingo · Bingo for Grades Three and Four · Football · Baseball · Developing Arithmetical Skills in Grade One · Social Activities that Develop Arithmetical Skills · The Meaning of Equations · Estimating Weights and Measures · Arithmetical Shuffleboard · Number Bowling · Basic Facts Chart · Using the Overhead Projector to Teach Arithmetic · Rules We Go By · Teaching Fractions by Overhead Projection · Projecting Manipulative Devices · Spin It · Stump the Panel Some Drilling Methods

Teaching Ideas That Make Learning Fun

Chapter 1. IDEAS TO USE IN TEACHING READING

SUMMARY OF TECHNIQUES

1

IDEAS TO USE IN TEACHING READING

Each elementary school system establishes its own objectives for a reading program. Although many of these objectives are the same from district to district, others differ in intent, scope, or wordage. There are, however, certain objectives which are considered as standard in all districts. These can be summarized as follows:

- To instill in each pupil a desire to read.
- To foster in pupils a thoughtful reading attitude.
- To develop accurate reading comprehension and interpretative skills.
- To permit each pupil to develop accuracy in word recognition and to enable independent interpretation of word forms.
- To develop a wide span of word recognition and a rapid reading rate.
- To develop proper rhythmic eye movement.

It is with these objectives in mind that the ideas for this chapter have been selected.

The reader will probably notice what appears to be an omis-

sion as the ideas are scanned. Many school districts regard
phonics as a primary technique in the teaching of reading. However, ideas concerning phonetic applications are not included in
this chapter, but are compiled in a separate chapter (2). This
organization is not a method of showing disagreement with those
who advocate phonics as an integral part of the reading program.
It is based on a desire to organize this book in a fashion which
will make it as easy as possible for the reader to use.

THE ILLUSTRATIVE BOOK REPORT:
AN IDEA THAT MOTIVATES

The illustrative book report is used to motivate students to
select books and read without knowingly being prompted. It
depends for its success upon the premise that youngsters tend
to follow the lead of popular classmates. Fortunately, in every
classroom, there is a leader or leaders upon whom the teacher
can rely to give the idea starting momentum.

Although the idea can begin as individual seat work, it will
probably soon broaden in scope. Students are advised: *"If you
wish,* you can prepare one book report each month (or two or
three—whichever the teacher desires) for extra credit."

Set aside a bulletin board for reports. The display can be
made more attractive by having a suitable block letter caption
placed atop the board. A sample caption is: "Books We Have
Enjoyed Reading."

Supply children who wish to do reports with sheets of 12" x
18" paper. Newsprint is suitable and inexpensive. Then instruct
them in the mechanics of preparing the reports. Of course, any
format you select will be suitable. What follows is an example
you may wish to use.

The paper is held horizontally. One-third to one-quarter of
the right-hand portion is folded over. The cover thus assumes
the appearance of the top part of a book jacket.

The children are asked to make a large, colorful picture of
an event they particularly enjoyed reading about for the front
portion of the jacket. Across the top of the fold-over leaf, they

should write the introductory phrase: "If you want to read a book about. . . ."

Beneath, they are then asked to list events they enjoyed or facts about a character or characters that impressed them. These descriptive sentences should be written in the sequence in which they appear in the book.

Beneath these sentences is written the phrase: "Then read. . . ." This is followed by the title of the book and the author's name. If the book is in the school or classroom library, a small asterisk can be placed at the top of the leaf.

The way in which you accept book reports and bring them to the attention of other students is important. You should, for example, make some appropriate remark to the class which will tend to motivate them to read the jacket, if not the book, when the jacket is tacked to the bulletin board. You might mention the title of the book, comment upon the exciting or comical scene which is portrayed by the cover illustration, or make a statement regarding how interesting the book appears from the description provided on the leaf.

Pupils should be allowed to go to the bulletin board at specified times during the day to examine the jackets.

One point must be emphasized in connection with this technique: no penalty should be meted out for mistakes made in spelling, grammar, or presentation. You should not, however, overlook errors, but bring them to the student's attention. The errors should not be overemphasized. In other words, the impression should not be given that the main purpose of the report is spelling or grammar.

In addition to being a valuable motivation technique, the illustrative book report is also a means of developing other language arts skills. It provides pupils with practice in writing sentences, titles, and names; in interpreting events and writing about them in concise sentence form; and in spelling and grammar. It further provides students with a chance to develop artistic skills.

The idea can be used from grades three to six. When used in upper grades where a more comprehensive report may be desired, additional writing space can be obtained by folding the sheet of paper in half. The entire inside portion can then be used for the report.

THE USE OF DRAWINGS TO FOSTER COMPREHENSION

The desire of children in the lower elementary grades to draw can be used to motivate them to read for comprehension and to allow vivid use of their imaginations.

Tell the class that they are going to read a story, which will be followed by a session during which they will illustrate an event from a list of events selected by the class at large. Follow the reading activity, which can be conducted either orally or silently, with a discussion that emphasizes and enumerates the sequence of events in the story. List this sequence on the blackboard.

Now, allow the children to select an event or events from the list that they wish to illustrate. The number of events the class selects depends on the time available for the activity.

Knowing that they eventually will be illustrating an event makes children read with more concentration and interest in order to obtain description and details they may otherwise overlook.

CHARACTERIZATION INCREASES THE DESIRE TO READ

An excellent method to increase the desire in students to read employs "play acting." The idea is particularly suited to upper elementary classes being introduced to novels.

Ask several pupils who have read the same book to act out a portion of that book for the rest of the class. Suggest to the acting pupils that they employ props and costumes to portray the characters. This will further encourage the other class members to read the same book.

Allow the imaginations of the actors to surpass the scene in the book only if the portrayal is consistent with the purpose of motivating the other students to read the book by making characters "come alive" before their eyes.

This same idea is useful in other subject areas. Students, for example, can act out events in the lives of famous persons in history.

"WHO AM I?"
A GAME TO BROADEN THE READING PROGRAM

Another idea for the upper elementary grades can be introduced later in the school year when a number of students have read several of the same books. The class is divided into two teams—the "acting group" and the "panel."

Members of the acting group portray a scene from a book, giving short clues which are difficult at first and become easier as the portrayal continues. The panel's task is to determine after each clue who the character or characters are and the title of the book.

If students on the panel provide the correct answers after the first clue, five points are awarded. Three points are given for providing the correct answers after the second clue. One point is awarded for giving the correct answers after the third clue. The two sides then change positions—the acting group becoming the panel, and the panel members becoming the actors.

After answers have been correctly given, the teacher, acting as moderator, can lead a discussion of the interpretations of characters and events provided by the acting group. This discussion is an additional learning experience.

This idea has the added benefit of motivating pupils who have not read certain books to read them. It may also provide an incentive for those who are lax to devote more time to reading, so they can take part in similar activities to be held in class at some future time.

TEACHING CHILDREN TO FOLLOW
DIRECTIONS

One of the most difficult problems the teacher faces is to get children to follow *exact* directions. As part of your reading program, you can initiate a game in which children are required to read and follow directions carefully, as well as to observe carefully, if they are to win the contest.

Write a group of directions on a strip of 3″ x 12″ oaktag. Compose as many groups on as many oaktag strips as you need to fill a particular time period. The following are ten examples of the types of directions you can compile (their wording is suitable for advanced pupils in grades two and three):

Oaktag Strip #1—Walk to the door. Tap three times. Skip back to your seat.

Oaktag Strip #2—Hop two times on your left foot. Clap your hands four times. Tap your right toe three times.

Oaktag Strip #3—Walk to your teacher. Shake her hand. Hop back to your seat on your right foot.

Oaktag Strip #4—Take a book. Walk to the teacher's desk. Put the book on the teacher's desk. Run back to your seat.

Oaktag Strip #5—Walk backwards to the blackboard. Print your name on the blackboard. Skip back to your desk.

Oaktag Strip #6—Walk around your desk twice. Clap your hands four times. Stamp your foot three times.

Oaktag Strip #7—Walk to the blackboard. Collect all the erasers. Put them in piles of two across the blackboard. Walk back to your seat.

Oaktag Strip #8—Hop to the door on your right foot. Open and close the door once each. Walk backwards to your seat.

Oaktag Strip #9—Run to the blackboard. Write the following on the board: 6 plus 3 equals 9. Erase what you have written. Walk back to your seat.

Oaktag Strip #10—Hop to the blackboard on your left foot. Put an eraser on your head. Walk all the way around the room. Put the eraser back. Skip to your seat.

To start the game, give one strip of directions to a child. He reads the directions, and then must follow them *exactly*. If he fails to comply with an instruction, he loses and is asked to sit down.

If he follows the directions as written, he is allowed to call on another pupil, asking him to tell exactly what was done. The only clue that can be given is the number of actions the player performed. For example, if the player was issued oaktag strip #1, he may say, "I did three things. What were they?"

The first child who can give the exact directions followed by the player receives the second oaktag strip to act out. The class may be divided into teams, if desired.

This technique can be used at any elementary grade level. In grades one to three, direction should be kept simple and few in number. In upper grades, direction can be made more numerous and difficult. Assure that wording of directions is in accordance with the reading level of the class. However, it is best to keep wording of directions on the independent rather than on the instructional reading level. In other words, directions should be worded so that no child will need your assistance in interpretation. This will assure that children who have difficulty in reading can participate in the game and learn how to follow directions.

COMPOSING SENTENCES HELPS
TO DEVELOP READING ABILITY

Children in the lower elementary grades who have difficulty reading usually can be helped by obtaining experience in composing sentences. When youngsters discover that sentences are not mysterious pitfalls, they achieve confidence in their ability and are often motivated to read independently and more extensively.

To help these children, you can employ oaktag strips on which are written sight words. The technique serves another purpose— to give you a general indication of the difficulties individual pupils are having.

Three groups of cards are prepared. The first group consists of the names of people and characters (Dick, Jane, Sally, Mother, Rabbit, Dog). One name is placed on a card.

The second group of cards consists of action words (run, skip, hop, puts, barks). Again, one word is put on a card.

The final group of cards consists of one short phrase per card (to the house, in the yard, to the car, at the man, up the street).

Each group contains the same number of cards A child is

allowed to take the group to his seat and arrange the cards into meaningful sentences. He writes these on a sheet of paper.

After finishing, allow the child to read each sentence to you. By being permitted to read aloud, the youngster can usually determine for himself whether a sentence makes good sense. Enabling him to discover his own mistakes is the primary benefit of this technique.

To facilitate your placement of word cards into proper groupings without having to read each one, apply a spot of color to the corner of each card. First group words, for instance, can be colored red; second group, blue; and third group, green.

RIDDLES REQUIRE THAT PUPILS
READ FOR COMPREHENSION

Youngsters enjoy riddles. This fact can be utilized to assist pupils in reading for comprehension, and also to determine which pupils are having difficulty.

Distribute drawing paper, pencils, and crayons to the children. Instruct them to fold the paper in half, thereby providing two sections on each side of the paper.

Have four riddles written on the blackboard. Each riddle should have the final word omitted. For example, riddles you can employ in grade three and four that can be taken from a lesson in science are as follows:

1. A tool which is a glass tube that we use to measure the temperature in a room or outside is called a _____.

2. When the mercury inside the tube is at 0°, we feel very cold. In cold weather, water will turn to _____.

3. When the mercury inside the tube is at 100°, we feel very hot. In hot weather, many people go to the beach and go _____.

4. Doctors use a tool of this sort to measure how warm a person is. When you are very warm, you are sick and have to go to _____.

Tell the children to write out each of the riddles on the bottom of each section of the paper; that is, one riddle per section. They should leave most of the section empty for an illustration. Now, instruct them to think what the answer might be. They should write the answer in the blank provided at the end of the sentence. Finally, have them illustrate each answer in the space provided.

AN ADVANCED RIDDLE ACTIVITY

As pupils progress in reading skills, riddles can be used to test their ability to read for interpretation. The riddles, however, should allow for more than one answer, unlike the preceding method which calls for one specific answer.

For example, a riddle that can be used in grade two is: "Jack has something in his pocket. It is something for a dog to eat. What could it be?"

It could, of course, be a number of things: a bone, dog biscuit, candy, etc. Ask the students to draw pictures of their answers. The purpose of drawing answers, as opposed to writing them out, is to allow students who have trouble in spelling to participate and not be inhibited. Keep in mind that this technique is an exercise in interpretation, and not in spelling.

GAME-TEACHING VOCABULARY

Vocabulary drill work, which is often tedious for teacher and pupils alike, can be made more enjoyable and a beneficial learning experience by use of imaginative techniques. Take, for example, the word game *ghost*. It might be "old hat" to you, but it isn't for the youngsters.

This game works nicely when you engage in vocabulary drill with a small group, while other students are doing independent seat work. Prepare a set of flash cards. On each write a vocabulary word taken from a recent reading lesson.

Hold up a card for the first player to see. He is required to pronounce the word correctly and to give its proper definition as it applies to the story he has read. If the player fails to fulfill the requirements, he is penalized with the letter *g*, and play passes to the next student. If a member of the group does not believe a player has provided the correct pronunciation or definition, he can challenge. However, he is required to provide his definition or pronunciation. An incorrect answer on his part draws a penalty.

When a child has been penalized wi.n the letters *g-h-o-s-t* (or any penalty word you wish to use,, he loses and the game is over. The pupil with the least number of penalty letters is the winner.

When this technique has been employed, teachers have found that children better retain definitions of assigned reading words. The game is also of value to you as a means of checking students for reading comprehension.

THE LADDER GAME:
A MULTI-PURPOSE READING TECHNIQUE

"During this school year, we are going to climb ladders right here in the classroom, just as firemen do or your father does when he works around the house."

Telling this to children in grades two and three at the beginning of a school term arouses immediate interest on their part. The purpose of the ladder-climbing game is to stimulate individual interest in reading, to provide an incentive to read, and to develop reading comprehension.

To initiate the project, prepare stories which you compose yourself, or which you clip from old workbooks and texts. Mount each story on a piece of oaktag. On the back of each oaktag card, write out questions that pertain to the story.

The oaktag cards are placed into groups of ten, according to reading difficulty, and are assigned a color code. Thus, there should be a group of ten red cards (red one, red two, red three, and so on), a group of ten blue cards, a group of ten green cards, and so forth. Each group is placed in its own box, with each box having a suitable means of identifying the color group. A colored square in one corner of the box, for example, which coincides with the color code of the cards in the box can be used. Boxes can be kept on the reading table.

To complete preparation for the technique, duplicate (mimeograph) a picture of a ladder for each child. Each rung of the ladder is numbered consecutively from one to ten. The children should be allowed to keep the pictures in their folders on the reading table.

Permit each child to work at his own rate of speed and on his own initiative. During independent activities, for example, youngsters can go to a box which contains a group of reading cards of a respective color, read the story from a card (or cards, if there is time), and answer the questions on the rear of the card (or cards).

However, children must progress in steps. There should be no skipping. A youngster must start with a particular colored group of his choice and do, in turn, each card in that group. Only when the youngster has finished all the cards in the group should he be allowed to proceed to the next, more difficult color group.

You will find that in selecting which group to start with pupils will tend to gravitate toward the group which is on a par with their reading level. If they begin a group and find it too difficult, they will leave it and return to a group of cards they can understand.

In doing the answers to questions, the pupil should write out the question exactly as it appears on the back of the card and then answer it. This gives the youngster practice in writing. For example, a question might appear as follows:

"John went to the (store) (movie) (doctor)."

The child should write out the complete sentence as it appears and then underline the answer he thinks applies. Depending upon the difficulty of the card, questions could be true-or-false, multiple choice, or interpretative types.

Of course, correct the papers. If only three or four questions have been asked on a card, all answers must be correct. If many questions are asked—six, seven, or more—allow the child to get one wrong. Those children who do not fulfill the requirements, as represented by how many questions they get wrong, should be told to re-read the card and re-do the paper.

As a pupil finishes each card, he colors in the rung of the ladder that corresponds to the card—for example, the first rung of the red ladder or the third rung of the blue ladder.

A word of caution: there will be a tendency on the part of children to "compare notes" and see where each stands in relation to the others. Take steps to minimize these competitive tendencies by stressing that the exercise is being done by each individual as individual work.

THE TRAIN GAME:
ANOTHER TECHNIQUE TO INCREASE
READING ACTIVITY

The fact that trains fascinate children can be put to good use in grades one to four.

"The more you read," you can say to them, "the more power you will give the locomotive, and the faster you will make the train go. For example, if you read one story, you will make the train go 10 miles an hour. If you read two stories, the train will go 20 miles an hour."

Provide each child with a mimeographed sheet to keep in his folder on the reading table. On the sheet is a picture of a locomotive, several train cars, and a caboose. All are coupled together.

A child selects a story book and reads one story at a time. As he finishes the story, he is given *yes-or-no* questions to answer. If he completes the requirement, he writes the title of the story on one of the train cars, which could then be colored to make the presentation more attractive and interesting. The title of the last story he reads from the book is placed on the caboose. The title of the book is placed on the locomotive when the child completes the work.

This exercise should be an independent reading activity, and supplementary textbooks contained in the classroom or school library should be used. The children are permitted to read at their own rate of speed. Pupils in grades three and four, and students in advanced reading groups in the second grade can be required to write a short paragraph about each story. This written exercise gives practice in interpretation of stories. In those grades where books are divided into units, the children should complete each unit before they are awarded a train car.

DEVELOPING SEQUENCE COMPREHENSION

To strengthen student understanding of story sequence and to provide exercise in finding the main thoughts of a story, have children in grades two to four make their own books.

Staple two or three sheets of paper together in book fashion— that is, stapled down the left-hand edge. Assign a story to each child and tell him to illustrate the story in sequence. Members of the top reading group should be required to write captions for the illustrations.

When pupils have completed the assignment, they should be allowed to tell their stories to other members of the class by showing and explaining the illustrations.

DEVELOPING STUDY HABITS

This exercise, which also helps to develop sequence comprehension, permits children to begin developing valuable study habits. Use a short story of no more than three or four pages. Number each paragraph in sequence. Have the children read the story and write in sequence one sentence that gives the main idea of each paragraph.

LET'S PLAY CARDS
(AND COMPREHEND AND INTERPRET)

An in-class card game, which children in grades two to four enjoy, will assist in developing reading comprehension and interpretive skills.

Prepare a stack of note cards. An ideal size is 3″ x 5″. Write an incomplete sentence on each, along with three word choices that complete the sentence. The child has to select the one word that best completes the sentence. This is an oral exercise.

Place the cards upside down in the middle of the reading table. Have each child, in turn, draw a card. He reads it and selects the word he thinks best for its completion. Ask the children as a group if this is the best word; if not, why it isn't. If the child's selection is considered best, he is awarded one point. If it isn't, he gets no points.

HELP THE AUTHOR

Select a story with which the class is not familiar. Explain that you will read the story, but you are going to need help.

You can state, "At times, I will stop in the middle of a sentence and call on you to see if you know what word comes next."

This simple idea permits children on any grade level who are having difficulty with word attack skills to develop confidence in their abilities. Point out at the close of the lesson that it is not difficult to read a story even though a person might not know all the words.

You should not pause too many times during presentation of the story to avoid breaking the students' trend of thought. This activity has the additional benefit, therefore, of getting children to concentrate as they read or listen, and of developing the skill of anticipating what is coming next.

DEVELOPING PRONUNCIATION SKILLS
BY MEANS OF OVERHEAD PROJECTION

If an overhead projector is available, you can use it to develop the pronunciation skills of students in grades one to four. The technique, however, is not limited to availability of a projector. A blackboard will serve as well.

"The name of the game we are going to play," you can explain, "is the stepping stone game. I will show you several words. Each word is a large rock in a pond. If you can tell me the word, you have gone forward one more step in crossing the pond. If you cannot tell me the word, it means you have slipped off the rock and have fallen into the water."

Transparencies can be prepared before class. Write several words on each transparency. Each word is enclosed in an oval to represent a rock. Around the "rocks" are several scribbly lines to represent water.

Student attention is particularly keen when the overhead projector is used, since children find the machine intriguing.

THE VALUE OF OVERHEAD PROJECTION

Since overhead projection has become a valuable tool for use in teaching, a summary of the benefits that can be realized by using this equipment in teaching reading is important. Keep in mind that the value of the projector depends primarily upon the teacher's imagination and the way in which she employs the equipment.

The following is a list of the benefits derived from use of the projector in the teaching of reading:

1. The overhead projector can save you time. New words, phrases, and sentences can be prepared before the class period. After use with one group of students, the transparencies can be filed for use later with other groups. Transparency material is permanent and cannot be damaged if properly prepared.

2. The projector is useful in developing eye span and for teaching the technique of left to right scansion. For example, expose a line from a story by means of the projector for a brief period. Then, remove the transparency, cover the line, or turn the projector off. Ask students to repeat the line. If they have difficulty, you can re-introduce the transparency and explain the proper way to read a sentence.

3. The projector is useful as a speed reading device. Reading time can be accurately controlled by simply turning the projector on and off.

4. The projector can be used as a testing device. For example, you can have students read silently from their texts. Questions concerning the assigned portion can be written out on a transparency. Place the transparency on the projector and use it as a guide for discussion or as a test. This is particularly suited for grades three to six.

5. The projector can be used in teaching the mechanics of reading, such as dictionary usage and phonics. Individual pupils can be allowed to work at the machine to develop skills in visual recognition of syllables, digraphs, compound words, and other work assigned as new or review.

6. The projector can be useful in grades one to three to give directions for worksheets that are to be completed as seatwork by the children. For example, a transparency can be made of an assigned page, and you can demonstrate the work to the entire class at one time by using projection. The students can then do the same work in their seats. Through projection, the children obtain a better understanding of what is expected of them, and they should be able to do work independently.

USE OF PUZZLES TO DEVELOP COMPREHENSION AND INTERPRETIVE SKILLS

Mimeograph sufficient copies of one story to accommodate the number of children in a reading group. Cut the mimeographed copies of the story into one-line strips and mix the strips together in a box. Put the box on the reading table. Each child has to sort out the story and arrange the strips in proper order on art paper.

Several variations of this idea can be used. For example, a contest can be held by dividing the group into two or more smaller groups. Place the story strips into separate boxes, one for each group. Each team works separately to unscramble the story. The first team to finish is the winner.

You could also duplicate more than one story and cut these into strips to make the assignment more difficult. Place the strips into one box. Students are required to unscramble more than one story.

This idea is suitable for use in grades three to six.

CROSSWORD PUZZLES

The value of crossword puzzles in teaching reading and other subjects should not be discounted. Puzzles are helpful in building vocabulary, developing dictionary skills, encouraging use of the dictionary, and in improving spelling.

Teachers have found that crossword puzzles are valuable in teaching social studies, science, and arithmetic. They can be used on any grade level and are excellent testing devices.

TEACHING HOMONYMS AND SYNONYMS

In teaching words that mean the opposite or the same in grades two to four, you can make use of the fact that children enjoy doing puzzles. For example, directions on mimeographed sheets passed out to each child may read: "Circle the word that means almost the same as the word or words that are under-lined."

Several typical sentences that can be used in grade three are as follows:

1. Jack ran <u>as fast as he could</u> and won the race.

    slowly   swiftly   evenly

2. He <u>uncovered</u> the box and saw the cookies.

    lifted   opened   took

3. <u>Brightly</u> colored balloons were everywhere.

    red   gaily   pretty

4. He left the house <u>unseen</u> and ran away.

    unhappy   unwilling   unnoticed

5. The fox is a <u>sly</u> animal.

    smart   silly   tricky

6. I would have done it <u>earlier,</u> but I was busy.

    sooner   faster   later

The technique not only provides training in reading, but has the additional benefit of providing exercise in other language skills, such as phonics. The method can also be used for testing.

TESTING STUDENTS FOR AN UNDERSTANDING OF IMPLIED MEANINGS

It can be determined if children are reading carefully enough to derive full meaning from a story or book.

Write a short, colorful paragraph about an event. Prepare several multiple choice questions about it, but to obtain the correct answer, children should have to probe the story for meaning.

The following is an example of such a paragraph and questions that can be used in grades three and four:

Story:

> The Hill family was ready to leave on a vacation trip. The car was packed with suitcases and fishing equipment. They left just as the sun was beginning to rise. They traveled across country roads and mountain roads.
>
> When they arrived at the vacation spot, they were tired, warm, and hungry. They could smell the food cooking in the big kitchen downstairs as they washed and got ready for a late supper.
>
> From the window of the room, Jill could see the dark shadows of the trees in the distant forest. The lake looked like a silver ribbon as she watched a boat glide silently across.

Questions:

1. This story takes place in
     winter—summer.
2. The trip was
     long—short.
3. They were staying in a
     small hotel—camp.
4. The weather was
     clear—cloudy.
5. It was _____ when they arrived.
     afternoon—evening
6. Jill could see the trees and the boat on the lake because
     the lights were on—it was a moonlit night.

A CHECK ON READING COMPREHENSION

This idea can be used in all elementary grades to determine which students are having difficulty in reading for comprehension. Have the children read a story and copy five sentences which you have written on the blackboard. Three of these sentences should be true statements of events in the story, and two should be incorrect statements. After reading the story, instruct the youngsters to put a check mark next to the correct sentences.

AN EXERCISE IN WORD RECOGNITION

Select several sentences from the day's story assignment and scramble up the words. Require the children to look for the correct sentences by re-reading the story. Then, have them unscramble the sentences and write them correctly.

A variation of this method can be employed. Have each child select a number of sentences from the day's story. Allow them to scramble the words themselves and write down the scrambled sentences. The students then exchange papers and each proceeds to re-read the story to find the correct sentences, which should be written on paper. This variation provides an additional exercise in careful writing. Pupils will be motivated to write more clearly and neatly when they know a classmate will be reading their work.

The technique is suitable for use in grades two to four. It has special value for students in slower reading groups.

BEGINNING DICTIONARY TRAINING

As a beginning dictionary exercise for pupils in grades one and two, and for middle and lower reading group students in grades three and four, have each child make his own vocabulary booklet. Use 6″ x 9″ arithmetic paper for *each* word. Words should come from vocabulary lists in the back of texts.

Establish three requirements for each word, as follows:

1. The word should be written in the upper right-hand corner of the sheet.
2. A sentence in which the word is used should be written along the bottom edge of the paper.

3. The child should be required to draw an illustration on the paper which pertains to the sentence. This requirement demonstrates if he understands the meaning of the word.

Each child can keep his papers arranged in alphabetical order in a folder. Eventually, you can have the youngsters insert these papers into individual vocabulary booklets.

PUT OUT THE FIRE
(A GAME FOR VOCABULARY DRILLWORK)

Prepare a poster showing a building that is on fire. Have "flames" shooting out the top window.

Draw in a ladder leading from the ground to the top window. Each rung of the ladder should have an adhesive-backed picture hook pasted over it. This poster can add meaning to vocabulary exercise and word recognition drill, and provide an incentive for youngsters in grades two to four.

Write words on small oaktag cards. Each card should have a hole punched in it, so the card can be put on a picture hook. Place a card on each picture hook.

During the drill, call upon one child at a time to determine how far up the ladder he can go to put out the fire. When the child falters or reaches the top, call upon another student.

ORAL READING EXERCISES

Oral reading exercises can be boring to those children who are not reading. The following are various ways of making this type of drillwork interesting for all:

• Instead of conducting oral reading exercises in the conventional manner (having one child read while others follow in their books), allow only the child *doing the reading* to have a book. Let the "listeners" know that they will be permitted to comment upon the oral presentation after the "reader" has finished. However, make sure that comments are kept in a positive vein, such as "he read very nicely," "the story was interesting," "I understood everything he read," and the like.

• Use stories with which children are not familiar. Have one child read, while others listen. Since the children have not heard or read the story, they will listen more attentively.

• If a tape recorder is available, use it. It is an excellent device for employment in oral reading exercise and holds a particular fascination for youngsters.

IN-CLASS PUPPET SHOW

Select a story which is particularly suitable for acting out with puppets, such as "Three Billy Goats Gruff." Have the children read the story. Then, assign parts to each and have them prepare stick puppets for a classroom puppet show. Students who are not given parts can be assigned to make scenery or operate sound effects.

Other classes can be invited to see the show, which gives your class experience in extending courtesy to others.

Chapter 2. TEACHING PHONICS
THE IDEA WAY

SUMMARY OF TECHNIQUES

2

TEACHING PHONICS THE
IDEA WAY

Phonics is the use of sounds in attacking new words. It does not involve a study of the parts of speech, such as action words (verbs). The only way in which phonics is combined with language studies at all is in simplifying words that contain prefixes and suffixes. It can be pointed out that when a prefix or suffix is removed from a word, a root word is left.

Phonics is an integral part of reading and should be taught as such. Although, for the purpose of organization, the two have been separated in this book, this chapter should be approached as a presentation of phonetic applications that are used in the teaching of reading. This chapter can, in reality, be considered as an extension of Chapter 1. It follows, therefore, that the objectives of the reading program which are outlined at the beginning of Chapter 1 are also the objectives of a phonics program. Again, let it be stressed that phonics and reading are one.

WORD ACTING FOR TEACHING ACTION WORDS

Acting out stories motivates children to read (see Chapter 1). Similarly, acting out single words assists children in grades one and two to learn action words.

Prepare a large number of flash cards. Write one action word on each, such as "hop," "talk," "cry," "jump," "sing," "sit," "walk," and "write."

Now, divide the class into two teams, and select a captain for each. The captain of one team takes a flash card from the pile and passes it to a team member who goes to the front of the room and acts out the word.

A member of the opposing team is called upon by the captain of the performing team to tell what the word is. If the student falters, the performing team is awarded a point. If the student knows the word, his team gets a point.

Play then passes to the other team. The team with the most points at the end of the lesson wins.

WHEEL OF WORDS TO TEACH CONSONANT BLENDS

A slide-rule instrument is useful in teaching mathematics. It also can be used to excellent advantage in teaching consonant blends in grades three to six.

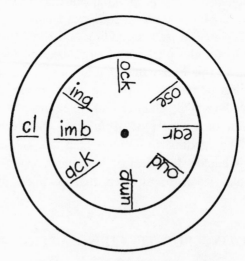

The Wheel of Words

Figure 2-1.

Cut two circles from oaktag, making one about one inch smaller than the other. Put the smaller wheel inside the larger wheel, and fasten the two together with a paper fastener. Thus, the small wheel will revolve inside the large wheel.

Write a consonant blend on the left side of the large wheel. Around the diameter of the small wheel write phonograms which, when combined with the consonant blend, will form words.

An example of a wheel for the blend *cl* is shown in Figure 2-1.

You can, of course, construct as many wheels as you desire for demonstrating additional consonant blends. However, it is a good idea to assign each student a consonant blend and have him make a wheel. He can then instruct fellow students in his consonant blend by use of the wheel.

PLAY DETECTIVE:
SOLVE THE VOWEL CRIME

Adding drama and suspense to a lesson adds to the learning experience. Can you imagine, for example, the interest you can evoke from children in grades two to four by announcing, "We are now going to be detectives."

You can continue by stating, "I am going to write five sentences on the blackboard. Next to each sentence will be a line. To solve the crime, you have to count the number of vowels in each sentence and put down that number on the line. Remember: do just one sentence at a time."

By use of this interest-provoking method, you can train youngsters to seek any sound, such as consonant blends, endings, long vowels, short vowels, and so forth. Examples of sentences in which pupils are asked to find vowels are as follows:

Solve the Vowel Crime

1. Jack and Jane went to the movie.   (10)
2. I like to go to the store with father.   ____
3. Sally gave Tom a yellow flower.   ____
4. Monday is the first day of school.   ____
5. It is snowing outside.   ____

"I'M THINKING OF SOMETHING"

This game is one that pupils in grades one to three find exciting. As an example of how the game would be played in grade one, a child would begin by saying to the class, "I'm thinking of something that starts with the letter *d*."

He would then provide one clue after another, with a five clue limit, if the class members cannot guess the answer. Examples of clues are as follows:

1. "Each child has one."
2. "It is a short word with four letters."
3. "Every child is using one now."

The answer is *desk*.

In grades two and three, clues may describe the word. For example, a clue for the above riddle would be, "it has a short *e* sound." If *flag* is the word the class is trying to find, a clue may be—"The word I'm thinking of begins with a consonant blend and has a short *a* sound."

The child who gives the correct answer is allowed to select the next word.

Objects selected for the game should be limited to a particular area, which is announced before the game begins. For example, objects can be limited to things in the classroom, or to things the children are wearing or possess.

VOWEL FINDING

Conduct a contest between class members who are divided into two teams. Each child writes out five sentences, leaving a vowel out of one of the words in each sentence. For example, "Jack sat on the st_p waiting for his sister."

Members of one team exchange papers with members of the opposing team. The object, of course, is to fill in the missing vowel.

To add more suspense to the contest and to provide yourself with a guide as to those children who are having difficulty with vowels, collect and correct the papers yourself. The suspense comes about, because children will not learn until the next day who won the competition. One point is awarded for each correct answer. The team scoring the most points is the winner.

This activity can be used effectively in grades one and two. In grade one, only one vowel should be omitted from a sentence. In grade two, two more vowels may be omitted.

HOMONYM HUNTING

To introduce students in the second and third grades to words having different meanings but the same pronunciation, list several homonyms on top of a duplicated sheet. For example, you could list the words *rode* and *road, reins* and *rains, sale* and *sail.*

Ask students to divide their papers into several sections. Then have them give a written description of each of the words, or have them draw a simple picture showing an illustration of what they believe the word depicts.

Word definitions do not have to be exact. All you should seek is association. An example of how a paper could look is shown in Figure 2-2.

Rode— to ride in a car	Road— a street
Sail— a boat	Sale— store
Rains— what comes from the sky	Reins— for a horse

Figure 2-2.

A variation of this technique is to distribute duplicated sheets which contain drawings depicting words on the homonym list. Also included on the sheet should be the list of words. The children are asked to associate a word from the list with each picture and write the correct word beneath the picture.

"PLAY BALL"—
REVIEWING PHONETIC SOUNDS

To add interest to a review lesson concerned with phonetic sounds in grades two to four, write various letter combinations on the blackboard. Arrange the class in a circle and place a large rubber ball in the center.

Assign a student to be "it." He comes to the center of the circle and selects a sound from the list. He tosses the ball to another student and says the sound.

The pupil to whom the ball is tossed must catch the ball and immediately speak a word using the sound. If he fulfills the requirement, he is now "it." If he fails to catch the ball or cannot give a word using the sound, he comes to the center of the circle and sits down. The original student remains "it." The student who missed remains in the center of the circle until another student fails to catch the ball or give a word using the sound. At that time, the former student can return to the group.

TRAINING IN IMPLIED MEANINGS

"Let us have a guessing game," you tell youngsters in grades two to five. "I have just passed out papers which contain a list of sentences. The first sentence of each group is a complete sentence and tells you something which a person is doing or something that is happening. The second sentence is another way of stating what that person is doing or what is happening. However, a word has been left out of the second sentence. I would like you to think of a word that means the same thing as that given in the first sentence and write it in the empty space. The clue to the missing word is to be found in the first sentence."

For example, the papers you pass out may contain sentences of the following nature:

1. Jane smiled as she walked to school.

   Jane was (<u>happy</u>) when she went to school.

2. Bob was hoping dinner would be served soon.

   Bob was (<u>hungry</u>) when he came home.

3. After working hard all day, Mr. Jones was happy to be home.

Mr. Jones was (<u>tired</u>) after working hard all day.

4. Ted was in a hurry to meet his friends.

Ted (<u>ran</u>) to meet his friends.

5. They took plenty of time walking on the slippery street.

They walked (<u>slowly</u>) on the slippery street.

6. As they reached the camp, they could see the light from the camp fire.

They arrived at the camp at (<u>night</u>).

7. Sue enjoyed the acts and animal tricks.

Sue enjoyed the (<u>circus</u>).

8. Bob watched the waves roll in.

Bob was at the (<u>seashore</u>).

When this idea is used in grades two and three, have a list of words on the top of each sheet passed to the children (or on the blackboard). From this list, students should be able to select the appropriate word for each sentence. In grades four and five, however, no clues should be provided.

You can also use this technique as an effective oral exercise. Give a sentence and call on a pupil to restate the sentence in another way, but with the same meaning. This variation can be used in grades three and four when dealing with words having opposite meanings.

THE WORD GAME

This game is suitable for use in the upper elementary grades. One word is selected as the "clue" word. Students are asked to find words hidden within the "clue" word within a specified time period.

For example, you may select the word *treasure* as the "clue" word.

"You will have 15 minutes to see how many words you can make using the word *treasure*," you may tell the class. "Don't

forget that you can only use the letters in the word *treasure,* and
you can only use each letter once if it appears once in *treasure.*
For instance, the word *treasure* has only one *t.* Therefore, you
can only use the letter *t* one time in each word you find. But
treasure has two *e's.* So, you can use *e* twice in each word you
find if you wish."

Examples of hidden words are as follows:

are	eat	set
as	err	star
at	rare	stare
ate	sat	sure
ease	seat	tease

A CARD GAME TO DETERMINE
PHONETIC UNDERSTANDING

Divide your class (grades one and two) or a group into two
teams and distribute to each pupil a stack of 2" x 3" cards, each
of which has a consonant written on it. All pupils should be
given the same number of cards and the same consonants should
be available to each.

Announce a word that begins with one of the consonants
you are using. The children hold up the card bearing the correct
beginning consonant. If all members of a team hold up the correct card, the team is awarded one point. If someone fails to
present the correct answer, no point is given.

This game can also be used in lessons concerned with ending
sounds and blends.

FOLDING CARDS TO EMPHASIZE
HOW WORDS CHANGE

Prepare a series of flash cards. On the front of each, write a
root word that can be changed by adding the letter *e* or an
ending. On the rear, write *e* or an ending. When the card is
folded, the ending or *e* should touch the root word. Figure 2-3
illustrates this.

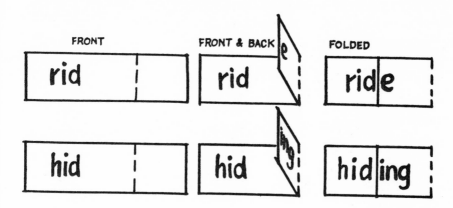

Figure 2-3.

Explain to the class (grades two to four) that words are often made from other words by adding an ending. Thus, the word with the ending has a different meaning from the word without an ending. Furthermore, stress that vowel sounds of words often change when endings are added to a word. You should demonstrate these two facts by using several of the prepared cards. Finally, tell students that the cards will be on the reading table for their use during independent work time.

FIND THE WORD

An independent phonics activity for the second and third grades involves a series of oaktag strips, each of which contains one sentence. A blank space should be left where a verb or noun has been omitted. Also prepare a stack of small cards with a noun or verb written on each.

Place the sentences and word cards on the reading table. Now, instruct the children in their use. Instructions can be changed daily or weekly, as you prefer. For example, you might say, "Today, you should find words that have short vowels to

complete the sentences." Tomorrow, you may wish to have the
youngsters look for words with long vowels or consonant blends.

Students go to the table and complete the sentences during
independent work periods. They write the sentences and their
answers on paper for checking by you.

USE OF CATALOGS AND MAGAZINES
IN THE TEACHING OF PHONICS

There is much the imaginative teacher can do in phonics work
by having students use old magazines and catalogs, especially
in the primary grades. For example, ask youngsters to bring a
magazine or catalog to school, and supply them with scissors,
paper, and paste. Using these materials, pupils can make individual phonics picture books over the course of a school year.

As they are studied in class, groupings can be included in the
books. Students clip pictures from the magazines and catalogs
having, for example, the following phonetic characteristics or
groupings:

1. Beginning consonant
2. Long vowel
3. Short vowel
4. Beginning consonant blend
5. Beginning digraph
6. Things for inside the house
7. Things for outside the house
8. Things for boys
9. Things for girls
10. Things for men
11. Things for ladies
12. Things for winter
13. Things for summer
14. Objects that have one syllable in the name
15. Objects that have two syllables in the name

Pictures should be grouped in their respective positions and
each group should be labeled.

SOUNDING OUT PICTURES

Have children in grades one and two fold drawing paper into thirds each way. In the lower right-hand corner of each square have them write a letter which has been studied in class. Compose an exact duplicate of what the children have on their papers on the blackboard. Papers and the example on the blackboard should appear as in Figure 2-4.

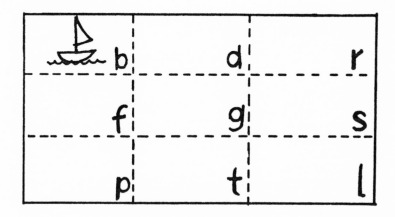

Figure 2-4.

Children can be instructed in this manner: "Look at the first square. What letter is this? That is right—*B*. Can you think of a word which has a beginning *B* sound? Yes—*boat*.

"I would like you to do this for each letter. Say the sound to yourself, select a name of an object that begins with that sound, and draw a picture of the object in the square."

When the children have finished the work, divide them into groups. Work with one group at a time while the remainder of the class is engaged in independent work. Call individual youngsters to the board. A child should say the name of the letter aloud, and the name of the object he has drawn on his paper that begins with the letter and sound. Then, allow him to draw the object in the respective square on the blackboard.

THE SYLLABLE GAME TEACHES
SYLLABLE FUNCTION

Teaching the function of syllables as they apply to word formation can be stressed to students in grades three to five by use of the syllable game. Divide the class into two teams and select a captain for each.

The captain of team one starts the game by saying, "I went to the grocery store and saw some ⸺." He calls upon a member of team two who is required to give an object he would find in a grocery store that has the number of syllables in its name as was decided upon before the game began. For example, if two syllable words are being emphasized, a child may answer "carrots," "apples," "cornflakes," "butter," "lettuce," and so forth. Naturally, words having one, two, or three syllables can be made the requirement.

If a child cannot think of an answer or fails to give a correct answer, the opposing team receives one point. No answer can be repeated. If it is, the child who first announced it raises his hand and scores a point for his team. The game ends when three children are forced to pass for lack of answers.

Other places that can be used in the game are school, farm, home, toy shop, zoo, and clothing store.

SIMON SAYS, CLASSROOM STYLE

Children in grades two to six can be trained to recognize particular sounds by means of this interesting technique. Suppose the phonograms being studied are "ack," "ing," and "old." These should be written on the board.

The attention of the children is drawn to the board. Then you state, "I am going to pronounce some words which have these phonograms in them. If the word has the 'ack' sound, I want you to hold up your left hand. If the word has the 'ing' sound, I want you to hold up your right hand. If it has the 'old' sound, I want you to put both hands on your shoulders. You must listen carefully in order to win the game."

Try one or two examples to see if the class has the idea. For example, you may pronounce the words *tack* and *bring*. Thus, the children should hold up their left hand and right hand, respectively.

"Now that you have the idea," you state, "we are going to make a game of this. Everyone will stand up. When I pronounce the word, those who do not give the correct signal will sit down. The last person standing will be the winner. I will go slow at first, but then I will go faster."

As children advance in grade, they can be asked to distinguish between homophones or diphthongs (for instance, *ay* and *ai,* or *oy* and *oi*) using this method.

A BEGINNING COMPOUND WORD EXERCISE

Duplicate a sheet for each member of the class which contains several incomplete sentences. A compound word is needed to complete each.

On another sheet, duplicate a list of single words in jumbled order. When two of these words are put together, they will make compound words to complete the sentences.

Provide youngsters with scissors and paste. Instruct them to cut out the words and put them together in the proper position in the sentence. Thus, the words should complete each sentence in a meaningful manner.

Examples of sentences are as follows:

1. The _____ rode the horses.
2. They sat around the _____ to keep warm.
3. At _____ we often see the moon.

Examples of words as they might appear in scrambled fashion on the sheet are as follows:

boy	fire
time	cow
night	camp

This exercise can be introduced in simplified form in the first two grades. Grades three to six can use it as compound words become more complex.

PUT AND TAKE:
A GAME FOR THE STUDY OF WORD PARTS

Place a variety of objects on a table. The names of the objects should contain phonograms being studied by the class. They might, for example, include a button (ut), pen (en), pencil (en), letter (et), jar (ar), apple (ap), map (ap), cup (up), bottle (ot), box (ox), hat (at), and so forth.

To start the game, divide the class into two teams. Pronounce a phonogram and call upon a member of one team. The student is given 15 seconds to find the object on the table whose name contains the phonogram. He picks it up, names the object, and writes the phonogram on the blackboard. He is then allowed to take the object to his seat.

If a child misses, an item is taken away from his team and placed back on the table. When all the objects are gone, the team which has the greatest number of them is the winner.

This game can be used from the second to the sixth grades.

A PROGRAM FOR DEVELOPMENT
OF WORD ATTACK SKILLS

An entire phonics lesson can be based on only 12 (or fewer) words. In fact, an entire phonics program can be based on 12 words.

Admittedly, employment of the technique presented here for development and review of word attack skills might be a difficult one for the teacher to master at first. However, once experience is obtained, she will find that the technique can be of invaluable assistance to students in development of word power.

Ideally, the method is used as part of a reading lesson. It therefore combines phonics, reading, and new vocabulary. The following is an example of how a lesson will evolve.

Select new words from a story. Keep each word in the exact phrase in which it was used in the story. This will give students simple context clues for the new words and will assist them in recognizing the complete phrases when they come across them later in the story.

Examples of phrases containing new words are as follows:

1. most important people
2. leader is forgotten
3. the horses trot
4. walked away slowly

These four phrases (12 words) that you write on the blackboard are the only ones employed in the lesson, which could last 20 minutes, one hour, or for as long as you desire. The lesson can be taken in steps. The following is an example:

1. Have a child read phrase one slowly.

2. Ask students what vowel sound is contained in the word *most* (answer: long *o*).

3. Have a child read phrase two slowly.

4. Ask students what the root word is of the word *leader* (answer: *lead*).

5. Ask students what vowel sound is contained in this root word (answer: long *e*).

6. Have a child read phrase three slowly.

7. Ask students what phonogram is contained in the word *trot* (answer: o̲t̲).

8. Using the phonogram o̲t̲ of the word *trot,* ask students to suggest consonants that can be used with the phonogram to make new words. The following are possibilities:

h<u>ot</u>	n<u>ot</u>
p<u>ot</u>	g<u>ot</u>
l<u>ot</u>	t<u>ot</u>

Note that the phonogram is underlined. It should also be underlined as you write each word on the blackboard to stress how to find phonograms in words.

9. Again using the phonogram ot of the word *trot,* ask students to suggest blends that can be used with the phonogram to make new words. The following are possibilities:

sp<u>ot</u>   bl<u>ot</u>   cl<u>ot</u>   sh<u>ot</u>

Again, the phonogram is *underlined.*

10. Have a child read phrase four slowly.

11. Ask students what the root word is of the word *slowly* (answer: *slow*).

12. Ask students what phonogram is contained in the root word *slow* (answer: *ow*).

13. Using the phonogram *ow,* repeat steps 8 and 9.

14. After each phrase is reviewed, ask students to look at the entire list and pick out the consonant blends they find. Underline them as they are pointed out. (Examples: trot, slowly.)

15. Ask students to find a compound word in any of the four phrases. As they do and call it out, write it on the blackboard and divide the compound word into its words. Examples are as follows:

    for/gotten   a/way

16. Ask students to find a suffix. (Example: slow<u>ly</u>.)

17. Ask students to find a prefix. (Example: <u>im</u>portant.)

18. Ask students to find the short vowel sounds in the phrases. As they do, put the short vowel symbol ($\smile$) over them.

19. Ask students to find the long vowel sounds in the phrases. As they do, put the long vowel symbol ($^-$) over them.

20. Ask students how they would divide several of the words into syllables, such as *im/por/tant, lead/er,* and *for/got/ten.* These are divided on the blackboard to emphasize syllabication.

As you can see, the phonetic uses of this technique are practically limitless in getting students to learn how to attack words. As this exercise is repeated time and again with new phrases from new stories, the students develop the skill of looking for phonograms, blends, vowel sounds, and so forth to help them attack new words on their own. The technique can be used throughout the elementary grades.

Chapter 3. IDEAS TO MAKE SPELLING INTERESTING

SUMMARY OF TECHNIQUES

3

IDEAS TO MAKE
SPELLING INTERESTING

Spelling is a tool for written expression. With this in mind, the following objectives for spelling instruction can be stated:

• Spelling should help each child meet his daily needs in written expression.

• It should teach children how to study words in order to be able to spell them.

• Spelling should develop a desire for accuracy in each child.

• It should encourage each child to use in his writing the words he has learned to spell.

• Finally, spelling should develop a sense of resourcefulness in each child to find words for which he has need.

The teaching and studying of spelling, however, need not be tedious or boring. To this end, this chapter explains techniques the teacher can use to make spelling interesting.

SPELLING CHARADES

When introduced into a spelling lesson on any grade level, the familiar and enjoyable game, charades, can be used to dispel the tediousness of drillwork. In addition to emphasizing the correct placement of symbols which comprise a word, spelling has the purpose of teaching a word's meaning or meanings. The purpose of spelling charades, therefore, is to implant in the minds of pupils an understanding of assigned terms by seeing these terms in action.

The word "airplane," for example, can be acted out by a member of the class. He might spread his arms as if they were wings and trot around the room while making a "whooshing" sound to denote a jet engine. Class members try to guess what the word is by the actions of the player.

If you wish, the class can be divided into teams and a point scoring system used.

MAKING SPELLING DRILL INTERESTING

Instead of conducting spelling drill in the conventional manner, introduce spelling questions into the lesson. These make spelling more interesting and tend to foster a desire in children to participate, which enhances the learning process. Phonetic exercises can be introduced simultaneously.

On the first day new words are covered, present them for study in the usual manner. The next day, however, instead of asking students to write each word a number of times, have the list of words on the blackboard and present questions which can be answered by use of one or more of the words.

The object of the exercise is to have children write the words as they would normally, but to do it in such a manner as to have the words implanted firmly in their minds. The following are examples of questions that can be employed:

Example 1: You may present this question: "I see a word in the spelling list that has a long *a* sound. Write it."

Example 2: You may state, "I see two words in the spelling list that begin with the same sound as the word *table*. Write them."

Example 3: You may have several words on the blackboard which are missing consonants or vowels. The object is to have the children write the word and fill in the missing letter.

Example 4: You may have several spelling words written on the blackboard with the letters scrambled. Youngsters are to unscramble the letters and write each word properly.

THE SPELLING TYPEWRITER GAME

Another game which can be used in grades one to four in place of drillwork is the spelling typewriter. Prepare alphabet cards to coincide with letters used in the week's spelling list. One letter is used per card. Pass out one card to each student.

Now, call out a spelling word. Those students who have the cards containing the letters in the word walk to the front of the room and stand in correct order so their letters spell the word.

This technique can also be used to reinforce phonetic principles by using derived words and substituting initial consonants. For example, suppose you had called out the word *hat,* and pupils possessing cards having the letters *h, a,* and *t* are in front of the class in correct order. Now, you can say, "I would like to see the word *sat.*" The child with the letter *h* sits down and the one with the letter *s* moves into correct position.

Furthermore, suppose the spelling word is *mat.* You may say, "I would like to see the word *mate* or *mating.*" The pupil with the letter *e* or those with *i, n,* and *g* move forward and stand in correct position.

"COMBINATION": A GAME WHICH MAKES STUDENTS SPELL

The class is divided into two teams, and a leader is selected for each team.

The leader presents a combination of two letters to the opposing team and asks that team to find a word in the current spelling list which uses the combination of letters. If the word given by the team is correct, one point is awarded. If more than one word is applicable and is given in addition, one point is awarded for each additional word presented.

The teams alternate questioning.

"DO YOU KNOW ME?"
A SPELLING GAME FOR GRADES ONE AND THREE

Select a student to begin the game. He spells a word from the word list, but does not pronounce it. Instead, he calls on a member of the class.

If the pupil called upon fails to pronounce the word correctly, another student is called on. The first youngster who pronounces the word properly becomes the next questioner.

EXPLORING WORDS

"Let's go exploring," you may say to your class (2nd to 4th) one day. "You have your word list before you. I am going to give a definition. Your job is to find the one word on the list that best fits the definition and write that word on your paper."

As each definition is presented, call on a student to write the word he selects as the correct one on the blackboard. The class then decides if the student has "explored" the correct word.

"ASSOCIATION": A GAME INSTEAD OF DRILL

This is another game you can use which alleviates the need for conventional spelling drillwork. Each word in a given spelling lesson will have something in common with other words in that lesson. The association may be a common beginning letter, letter combination, prefixes, suffixes, the identical number of letters, the same consonant blend, or what have you.

Pupils are asked to find as many pairs of words as they can for each particular association within a specified time period and list them on paper. They can then be called to the blackboard and present them. The remainder of the class can participate by citing others they have found.

WORD-O

"Your parents often play *bingo*," you tell your students one day. "You and I are going to play a similar game called *word-o*.

"Each of you has a sheet of paper (8½" x 10"). Fold it like I am doing into 16 equal parts." (Demonstrate, if necessary.)

"Now, write carefully one word into each space from the current spelling lesson and from your list of review words. When you finish, you should have 16 words."

Collect the papers and redistribute them so no student has his own paper. Supply each child with pieces of cardboard or paper discs.

Now, call out words from your master list. The game proceeds as does bingo, with the first student to cover applicable squares holding up his hand and announcing, *"word-o."*

THE ERASER GAME

This game combines conventional spelling drillwork with an activity for students in grades one to four. Have children orally spell new spelling words. As they do, list the words on the blackboard.

Now, call on a pupil to come to the board and erase one of the words while other students have their heads down. The child who erased the word calls on another to spell the missing word. The first child who successfully spells the word becomes the next "eraser."

WORD DOMINOES

The object of this spelling game is to use letters to build words. This activity is a small group exercise for grades three to six.

Each child is given ten cards, each of which contains one letter. A batch of cards, each containing one letter, is placed in the center of the group. The group is formed into a semicircle.

A pupil starts the game by writing the letter from one of his cards on the blackboard. He places the card into a discard pile. The next child selects an applicable letter from his cards and writes it on the board next to the first letter. If the student does not have a letter that fits, he draws one from the pile in the center. As each word is completed, it is erased and a new one is started. However, the same word may not be used again.

The first child to be rid of all his cards is the winner.

SPELLING AS PART OF READING

Many educators are now stressing the desirability of presenting spelling words in story form. New words should be used with words previously studied as part of a paragraph or two. This method of presenting new words provides students with an opportunity to observe words in action. Words, therefore, begin to have more meaning to youngsters.

THE TOUCHING GAME

This game is useful as a small group activity in the second and third grades. Children in the group place their hands behind them. You hand the first student an object, but he is not permitted to look at it. He is supposed to name the object and spell the name. If he does, another object is handed to the next student. If the first pupil cannot name and spell the object, it is passed to the second student. Objects should have names that have been studied in spelling lessons.

One point is awarded for correctly naming the object, and a second point is given if the student spells it correctly.

WORD ANALYSIS

Compile a list of words from the master spelling list, but avoid a lengthy list.

There are many word analysis games you can employ using these words. Each of these exercises contributes to an understanding of word elements and benefits children in reading as well as in spelling. The following is a compilation of exercises that you may want to introduce:

- Find the little word in a big word.
- Find all the words that have the same little word in them.
- Find all the words that begin with the same sound.

- Find words that sound like each other (rhyme); for example, *hide* and *side*.
- Put in the missing letter; for example, ho_se (house).
- Tell which word has been erased from the list.
- Make new words by putting different letters in front of small words; for example, *s*-at.
- Write words that begin with the same consonants.
- Write in the missing word in a sentence; for example, "Tom went with his _____ to the store." (sister)
- Find words that have almost the same meaning; for example, *spot* and *stain*.
- Find words that have opposite meanings; for example, *bright—dull*.
- Find the word that has a particular meaning; for example, find the word that means something to eat (bread).
- Pick out known parts of new words; for example, *some*day, *after*math, *be*side, par*take*.
- Identify rhyming words; for example, *man—fan, like— bike, sight—might*.
- Locate words with double consonants or double vowels.
- Add suffixes to make new words.
- Add prefixes to make new words.

REVIEW SPELLING BY PLAYING BASEBALL

By making a spelling review into an occasional "baseball game," you will capture the interest of your third to sixth grade class. Words that may not have been learned before will now be retained in many cases.

Divide the class into two teams (home team and visitors). Appoint a student as scorekeeper. He has the job of keeping track of outs and runs scored.

Designate one corner of the room as home base. The corner nearest the blackboard is best. The remaining three corners, going counterclockwise from home base, are first, second, and third bases.

The first student, a member of the visiting team, steps to the blackboard. You call out a word from the review list. The "batter" is to pronounce the word and write it on the blackboard. If he does both correctly, he goes to first base. If he fails to pronounce or spell the word properly, he is called out and takes his seat.

The next student comes to home base. If he gets a "hit" and there is a student on first base, the latter advances to second while the former goes to first base. When a third batter gets on base, the two already on base advance one base each, and so forth.

Each team stays at bat until there are three outs. To make sure the game ends fairly without complaint from students, judge your time to allow each team the same number of turns at bat. If you have a class of exceptional spellers, reduce the number of outs for each team to two or even one.

TRACK MEET

Here is another "sporting event" you can use in grades three to six to further the study of spelling words.

A leader is appointed in each row. Each leader is supplied with a list of spelling words and pronounces the first word from it when you state, "go." The first student in each row (not the leader) rushes to the blackboard and writes the word as quickly as he can. If he misspells the word the next student in the row must correct it. If he also misses, then the next speller must see that it is corrected. It is the leader's responsibility to assure that no incorrect word is allowed to pass. If it is, the team cannot win the game although it may complete its list before the other teams.

The team that completes its list correctly before the others wins the relay. To avoid copying, each leader is supplied with a different list of words. The lists can be exchanged and play resumed if there is time.

To get full benefit from the lesson, students should be told the day previous to the "relay race" that it will be held the next day. Since no student likes to be the cause of his team failing, pupils will usually study the entire word list the night before the game.

SPELL AND BOUNCE

Children in grades one to three will enjoy this game and learn to spell at the same time. As he spells a word, a youngster bounces a rubber ball one time for each letter in the word.

If he spells the word correctly the first time, he tosses the ball to the next player, pronouncing a spelling word from the assigned words of the day or week as he does. The new player then must spell the word and bounce the ball. In order to participate in the game, therefore, children must be able to retain assigned words in their minds, pronounce them properly, and be able to spell them.

If a player misspells a word, he is given a second opportunity. If he again misses, he sits down and play is resumed by the next student. If a player cannot think of a word from the spelling list, he too must sit down. The teacher tosses the ball to the next student, pronouncing an assigned word. The last player left standing is the winner.

This game is one for small groups of five to seven children, while other students are engaged in independent seat work.

Chapter 4. HOW TO DEVELOP A CHILD'S ABILITY TO WRITE

SUMMARY OF TECHNIQUES

4

HOW TO DEVELOP A
CHILD'S ABILITY TO WRITE

The stimulation of written language ability can be furthered by the teacher through classroom activities. Development of these abilities is an even more deliberate process than the development of oral expression.

Programs in written language are generally designed to attain the following goals:

- To assist children in an understanding of how written expression can serve them by creating situations in the classroom that call for writing.
- To encourage children to express themselves freely in writing.
- To teach children to employ correct form in written expression.
- To develop gradual growth in writing by assisting children to write for an increasing number of purposes with an increasing sense of independence.

TAPPING THE CREATIVE WRITING POTENTIAL

Pupils start to form good writing habits in grades two to four. Some youngsters, even at this early age, prepare stories that show a great deal of imagination and creativity. You can put into use the following technique to tap this vast potential:

Begin with a reading assignment in which children are asked to read a book of humorous, make-believe stories, which explain why certain things are as they are. Following completion of the book, ask children to write make-believe stories based on principles they have learned and discussed in science. Suggest they use the imaginative book they have just read as an example. Immediately, three disciplines are used to promulgate practice in creative writing: reading, science and, of course, writing.

"When all stories have been completed," you can state, "we shall make a book of them and keep it in the class for your parents, classmates, and other teachers to read."

Knowing that their stories will be "published" adds another inducement, but you should stress that none of the stories will be corrected or graded.

The following excerpts, printed here as they were written (with grammatical and spelling errors), demonstrate the potential creative writing talents that can be fostered. These stories were written by second graders:

Why We Have Night and Day
by Susan

Once about 50 million years ago the sky was full of monsters of all kinds. One of them was greenish-purple and he was the meanest, too. His tail was so-o-o-o big and thick it covered half the earth. It was so dark that the people called it night. One day the monster began to breathe fire. It was so bright that people called it day. Even though he did it to be mean, people learned to like day and night.

A Story
by Steven

Once there was a giant that had a yo-yo with the sun on the end of it. The giant loved to play with his yo-yo. When the yo-yo went up the sun came out and when the yo-yo went down it was dark. When he got tired the days got longer. When he went faster the days got shorter.

Why It Snows

by Judy

Once, a long time ago there was a little town called Hot Town. That was it's name because it was so-o-o-o-o-o Hot all the time. One night the man in the moon got out his shaving cream and started to shave. All of a sudden the shaving cream got cold and started to spray all over. It even sprayed on Hot Town. The peaple in Hot Town liked this wonderful white cold stuff so they called it snow. From that day to this the man in the moon's shaving cream has fallen to earth to cool peaple off.

If you wish, have children illustrate their stories.

COMBINING WRITING AND SPEAKING

To begin this exercise, which can be used on any elementary grade level, tell the class, "I would like you to close your eyes and think of something you want more than anything else. But it must be something that is possible to get."

After giving students several seconds to think, state this: "Now, I would like you to write down on paper what you are thinking of. I would like you to describe it using only three words. I would then like you to tell what you would do with it, using only two sentences. Finally, I would like you to write a paragraph explaining why you believe you should have it."

When students complete their papers, call upon several to give an oral report, using their papers as a guide. Explain that in giving the report, they can expand upon the "notes" they have written on their papers.

DEVELOPING HANDWRITING
IN GRADES TWO TO SIX

Let each child keep a handwriting notebook. During the first week of school, they should make the following entry on the first page:

Writing

Name:——————————————— Date:————————————

"This is my best handwriting on this date."

Each month thereafter until the end of school, give an assignment to be written into the notebook "in your very best handwriting." Children will be able to see their progress. In addition, you will be able to use the notebooks as an example to some children that other written work they are doing is not being done in their best handwriting.

A BEGINNING EXERCISE IN TENSES

Children usually begin the practice of tenses halfway through grade one. This idea, which is included here because tense formation is an integral part of writing, can be used when working with smaller groups. It will permit you to concentrate your efforts on those pupils who have the most difficulty with tenses.

Distribute two cards to each child. On one card is the present tense of a verb; on the other is the past tense. This, of course, can vary as more work is done with tenses. For example, future and active tenses can be used later on.

Form the group into a semicircle in front of the blackboard, and write two sentences on the board which apply to one pair of words. For instance, if the words are "tell—told," the sentences might be as follows:

"I can't ——— you the secret."

"John ——— Mary he was going to the store."

Note that the applicable word is omitted from each sentence.

The child with the correct set of cards comes to the board and holds the cards in the proper spaces to complete sentences. He is not told to come to the board unless he makes no movement. The child reads each sentence after completing it.

You can retain the cards and sentences for use in lessons with other groups of students.

CLASSROOM POSTAL SERVICE

A classroom post office in grades three to six gives students exercise in the proper writing of letters and in good writing per se. A cardboard carton may be decorated and used as the mailbox, and students can alternate at being the postman.

During free-time activities or, if you wish, during a time period specifically set aside for the activity (perhaps weekly), students are allowed to write letters to fellow students and "mail" them in a properly addressed envelope. If the envelope is not properly addressed or the postman cannot read the writing, the letter is put into the "dead letter" pile. The envelope address should look like the one in Figure 4-1.

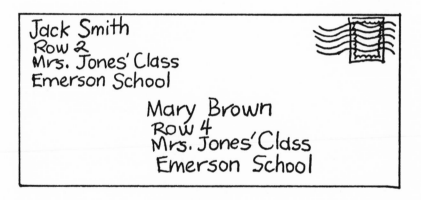

Figure 4-1.

While the letters are being written, walk among students and offer suggestions or answer questions about letter writing. Do not, however, collect letters or make an attempt to read them unless a student requests it. Stress that a letter between two people is private.

The postman empties the mailbox as often as you decide and distributes letters. A good time to do this is near the end of a school day, so students can read their letters at home.

RECORD KEEPING

This third to sixth grade writing activity can be an individual or group project. Actually, it is nothing more than assigning pupils to the maintenance of a diary of classroom events, such as the growth of an in-class garden, activities surrounding a classroom pet, or a record of special events. Records can be illustrated by the record keepers. They can eventually be made into a class yearbook.

NEWSPAPER WORK

One of the most effective techniques in stimulating students to write is to let them act as newspaper reporters and editors. Establish a class newspaper which can be published monthly, bimonthly, or as often as you wish.

Students can write about anything which pertains to the classroom or about class members. Topics can include everyday room news, classroom helpers for the period, original poems and stories, good citizen rules, news of pupil summer and holiday activities, stories about pupils' pets, and important dates to remember (PTA meetings, holidays, and such matters).

The physical makeup of the newspaper can vary. It can be mimeographed, so each child can have his own copy. If this is not feasible, a portion of the bulletin board can be set aside for the paper.

This technique is suitable for any elementary grade level, but is particularly valuable when students begin to write more prolifically, as halfway through grade two.

WRITE A STORY

To begin this voluntary, free-time activity, gather a set of pictures which portray action suitable for story writing. Place them on a reading table or other accessible table. A number is assigned to each picture.

The purpose of the number is to provide some means of

organization to the project. Each child may start with a particular picture (you record the number), but may not proceed to another picture until he completes the one he first selected.

You should emphasize at the outset that stories will not be corrected. This is done to allow full use of a child's imagination and to develop a desire to write creatively without being stifled by worry over grammar and spelling. Youngsters may, if they wish, illustrate their stories, and they should be given the opportunity to read them to the class if they wish.

The fact that participation in the project is a "treat" must be made perfectly clear to the children. You may, for example, tell pupils that they can compile the stories they write as a story booklet to present as a gift to their mothers on Mother's Day or to their fathers on Father's Day.

The technique is valuable in developing creative writing skills in pupils in grades two to four. In the third and fourth grades, you can hold a critique with each child as he completes his stories, giving suggestions about story organization and style.

A BEGINNING WRITING EXERCISE
FOR GRADES ONE AND TWO

Establishing a solid foundation for writing skills is an important aspect in grades one and two. One exercise you can use involves dividing the blackboard into four sections. In each section, draw or tape an illustration of a prepositional phrase. For example, pictures might show a ball *under* a table, a pot *on* a stove, a car *in* a garage, and the moon *above* a house.

Write a question in each box. For example, "Where is the ball?" "Where is the pot?" "Where is the car?" "Where is the moon?"

Distribute paper to the children and instruct them to fold it in half each way, making four sections. Then, ask them to draw the pictures and copy questions just as they appear on the blackboard.

Proceeding with the exercise, you can tell the children, "Here we see a ball and a table. Where is the ball?"

Call on a student and ask him to answer the question using

a *complete* sentence. When the child states, "the ball is under the table," or words to that effect, write the sentence into the appropriate box on the blackboard. Ask children to do the same on their papers.

Finally, tell pupils to complete the remainder of the work, but emphasize that complete sentences must be used in answering the questions.

A ONE MINUTE STORY GAME

Tell the class (grades three to six) that the object of the game is to pick up a story where a classmate has left off. Use the blackboard.

Call on the first child, who comes to the board and begins to write a story. At the end of one minute, stop him although he may be in the middle of a sentence. Call on a second child. He is required to pick up where the first child left off. He, too, has one minute to write.

The exercise can be extended to include as many students as you wish. However, ten should be the limit. The last pupil called upon should be required to write a conclusion to the story. You can then call upon another student to read the story aloud.

Stress to the class that they must watch the board carefully and be thinking of what they might write if called on.

AN IN-CLASS ESSAY CONTEST

Essay contests in which third to sixth grade students are contestants and judges provide both an incentive to writing and practice in reading. This should be a free-time, voluntary activity.

Students who wish to participate select a topic, write an essay about it within a word limit established beforehand, and submit them to a panel of classmate judges. Judges select first, second, and third prize winners. They may even wish to make "ribbons" for prize winners and have the ribbons displayed on the bulletin board along with the winning essays. You should allocate class time for the reading of winning essays.

USING OVERHEAD PROJECTION TO TEACH WRITING

If an overhead projector is available, it can serve as a valuable tool in the teaching of written expression in grades four to six. Classroom-wide critiques of student compositions and stories can be held. In addition, the best writing can also be projected and discussed as to style, organization, and sentence structure. Many pupils are motivated to improve the quality of their work after having interesting writing brought to their attention.

For example, suppose you display work done by several students. Using the overhead projector, the stories are enlarged and projected for all in the class to see at one time. Grease pencil is used to underline or circle errors. Either you can do this, or you can call on students to provide a critical analysis of their own or classmates' papers. Such writing faults as the following can be pointed out:

- Misplaced modifiers
- Improper use of capitalization
- Omission of commas
- Improper agreement of subject and predicate
- Incorrect spelling
- Misuse of the period
- Incomplete or awkward sentence structure

Your overhead projector may also be used in a study and analysis of penmanship, which is part of the writing experience. You can show the entire class what good penmanship looks like and how to form letters.

USING COMIC STRIPS VIA PROJECTION TO TEACH WRITING

Comic strips with words removed can form the basis of creative writing experiences in grades three to six. Prepare a transparency by first clipping a comic strip from a newspaper and blocking out the narrative contained in the balloons with opaque white paper. The setup is then reproduced on transparency material and the finished transparency is projected.

The comic strip is an effective aid in teaching narrative-type exposition. Students gain experience and knowledge in writing direct quotations, in paragraphing when speakers change, and in combining description with direct quotatons.

As a lesson progresses, the class can write a story in paragraph form based on the comic strip. The mechanics involved in this type of writing should, of course, be explained beforehand. Since comic strips without narrative are nondescript and open-ended pupils can let their imaginations run rampant.

Chapter 5. IDEAS FOR DEVELOPMENT OF ORAL EXPRESSION

SUMMARY OF TECHNIQUES

5

IDEAS FOR
DEVELOPMENT OF ORAL
EXPRESSION

In developing each child's ability to orally express himself, teachers should set an example. They should utilize correct grammatical forms, clear enunciation, and good pronunciation. In addition, teachers should guard against use of incorrect speech by children. A child should be corrected without being made to feel self-conscious. Children should be encouraged to reply to questions in simple, but complete sentences.

The tendency of children to use slang expressions can be gradually overcome through the use of games, by the teacher's example, by having a child repeat in correct form the statement in which a slang expression has been used, and by emphasizing to the child a better way of expressing the same idea without the use of slang.

Development of a pleasing voice can be encouraged by the teacher's example. She should always speak in a well-modulated voice. Children have to be reminded frequently that other people will be able to hear them if they speak in a natural voice.

Free, spontaneous conversations during work and play periods should be encouraged to prepare students for conversation periods. To stimulate a desire and need to communicate and express one's self, conversations can concern a multitude of subjects which are interesting to a child, such as pets, plants, experiences at home, play experiences, and television programs.

ESTABLISHING SPEAKING STANDARDS

As children progress into higher grades and their ability to speak develops, they should be urged to write speeches for delivery to an audience. These speeches can deal with subjects being presented in class periods, or with outside interests.

It is advisable that you establish a set of standards for the class. These have a dual purpose:

1. To develop in children a sense of confidence in addressing an audience.

2. To develop a sense of courtesy and respect when part of an audience.

These standards, which apply to pupils in grades four to six as well as to public speakers of all ages, can take the following form:

- Plan the talk.
- Avoid unpleasant topics.
- Face the audience and look directly at them.
- Avoid distracting and improper mannerisms of speech and posture.
- Make sure the audience can see all illustrative matter you are presenting as part of your talk.
- Make the talk long enough to hold the audience's attention, but not so long as to bore them.
- Be aware of and sensitive to audience reaction.

WHAT THE TEACHER AND CHILD
SHOULD EXPECT

The first three school years are critical in the development of the child's ability to express himself orally. General ideas of what the teacher and child should expect at the end of grades one, two, and three have been compiled. They are presented here for your information.

At the end of grade one, a child should have learned to choose desirable topics for conversation. He should be taking part in group discussion and be able to maintain the point under discussion. He should be able to retell or dramatize a simple story. He should speak naturally and easily to a group. He should have a desire to tell others about enjoyable experiences. He should be able to speak so others can hear and understand. Finally, he should listen when others are speaking.

By the end of grade two, the child should have improved his ability to choose desirable conversational topics. He should be participating in group discussions in a more intelligent manner. He should have progressed in his ability to retell and dramatize stories, and in his ability to speak naturally before his classmates. He should have developed a wider vocabulary, and his ability to address an audience should have improved. Finally, he should have a growing consciousness of correct forms of speech and know how to express himself in sentences.

At the end of grade three, the child should be more discriminating in choosing topics based on his experiences and informational reading. He should be taking an active part in group discussions and show some leadership traits. His dramatization and retelling of stories should be effective, and he should be able to express ideas in more clear and varied ways. He should be able to use concrete and vivid words instead of trite expressions, and he should have the ability to speak in a pleasing voice.

Furthermore, he should be conscious of his vocabulary and be continually adding to it. He should have a greater ability to recognize and use correct forms of speech, and he should plan his talks so they include good beginning and ending sentences. He should be showing some ability in organizing his thoughts, and he should be using aids to develop his word power, such as dictionaries and a glossary. At this juncture, a child should have a growing sense of audience reaction.

WORKING WITH PUPPETS

Students who are shy when speaking before an audience will often speak up clearly and without inhibition if they are hidden. Puppet shows permit this and eventually give shy students in grades three to six sufficient confidence to address groups "in person."

Puppets are easily made. Those of the stick type are cartoon characters that are cut out and painted or colored, and then stapled to stiff cardboard.

Puppets can also be made from paper bags. The character's face is drawn on one side of the bag, and the back of its head on the other side. The bag is loosely stuffed with crumpled paper to give it body, and the puppet is manipulated by hand.

A table turned on its side makes an adequate stage. Youngsters hide behind it and elevate the puppet, so that only the puppet is revealed to the audience. Scripts for a show can be taken from a book, or from original writings by students or teacher.

SPEAKING AND WRITING PROGRESS CHART

A chart showing individual pupil progress is a valuable tool. Children are particularly anxious to get a "star" or keep their names out of an error column.

This device can be used on any elementary grade level to stress the necessity of avoiding errors in speaking and writing. Since placing all the children's names on one chart is not possible, several charts should be made. You can use reading groupings, alphabetical groupings, or indiscriminate groupings as a basis for each chart. See Figure 5-1.

Additional entries to each chart can be made as individual pupils make errors that you correct. For example, you may say, "No, Bill. The word is not 'learn,' but 'teach.' This is a good one to add to our chart."

Letter designations, such as S, O, N, and D, stand for the month. Numerals beside each monthly designation indicate how many times during the month the child made the same error. If he does not make an error during a month that was made the previous month, the monthly designation is included on the chart and the symbol + is placed next to it. This symbol means that the child is improving. If he does not make the same error for two consecutive months, the symbol I (alone) is entered. This means that the child has improved considerably.

Speaking and Writing Progress Chart						
Errors	Mary	Jane	Jack	Dick	Ruth	Ted
"ain't"				$S^4O^2D^+$		
"done" for "did"			$S'O^+ID^2$			
"don't" for "doesn't"		S^4O^5N'				
"busted" for "broke", "broken"						
"learn" for "teach"				$S'O^+I$		
"I and you"						$O'N^+D^2$
"this here"					$N'D^+$	

Figure 5-1.

SILENT "SPEAKING" IMPROVES ENUNCIATION

An exercise that causes students in grades three to six to guess at something is usually interesting to them. A typical example is lip reading, which has the benefit of improving enunciation of the student who is "speaking."

Begin by demonstrating how carefully one must "speak" words when expressing one's self silently. Impress how lips must be formed when no sound is uttered. Have pupils do the same.

This technique can be transformed into a game. Divide a group into two teams. Have a pupil from one team begin the game by silently enunciating a short sentence. He should do this at a rate of speed which permits each word to be orally pronounced by members of the opposing team. A scoring system can be established.

FOSTERING ORAL EXPRESSION

To foster good speaking habits in elementary grade students, a daily exercise can be an announcement period. Several minutes can be set aside each day during which announcements pertaining to the school or class can be given. Students can take turns being the announcer for the day (or week).

The activity can be transformed into a daily radio news program, if you wish. The announcer of the day can relate such events as birthdays, illnesses, the loss of personal belongings, class functions, school functions, library hours, lunchroom menu, and out-of-school happenings that would be of interest to class members, such as a television program which youngsters may wish to watch that evening.

Chapter 6. IDEAS TO USE IN DEVELOPING LISTENING ABILITY

SUMMARY OF TECHNIQUES

6

IDEAS TO USE IN
DEVELOPING LISTENING ABILITY

Listening, an integral part of oral communication, may be defined as the attention and interpretation given to sounds or groups of sounds that arouse curiosity. Children do not listen to all they are told, and a child's interest thus becomes an important aspect in teaching him to listen. This factor poses a particular problem for you, the teacher.

You must recognize and stimulate the child's curiosity. You must also promote experiences that afford an opportunity to listen.

Listening can be classified into the following groupings:

- Listening for enjoyment
- Listening to obtain information and ideas
- Listening for direction
- Listening as a means of gaining social approval.

You should provide careful guidance to help children build a foundation for intelligent listening, to help them evaluate what they hear, and to use the information they obtain in forming judgments and reaching conclusions.

When planning activities for listening development, keep in

mind that such activities should be conducted in a friendly, re-laxed atmosphere which will encourage good listening habits. You have at your disposal several devices that can be used for this purpose. These include stories, poems, music, recordings, radio, and tape recorders. Naturally, some children in developing listening ability need the opportunity to listen in small groups for short periods before joining larger groups in assemblies.

WAYS TO EVALUATE DEVELOPMENT
OF LISTENING ABILITY

The following are suggestions for evaluating a child's listening ability development:

• Determine the child's needs for development by presenting him with simple directions to follow. Give directions one time only and test results. Then, repeat the experience and note im-provements or lack thereof.

• Play games in which the need for listening and the necessity for following directions are important.

• Send children on errands without providing them with a re-minder list.

• Conduct informal conversations with children and observe their listening habits and courtesy. Keep progress records.

• Recall important events and keep a progress record of how children retain information.

• Nurture the desire in children to listen by discussing in-teresting radio programs, newscasts, advertisements, and the like.

• Test the ability of children to listen by using recordings. Play a recording for yourself first, noting details. Then play it for students, discuss it, and replay it. Children should then be given the opportunity to evaluate the recording.

• Offer children opportunities to grow in critical thinking by letting them judge artistic concepts, reasoned conclusions, value-less items, the facts of a situation, and what is important.

• Keep listening logs. For example, pupils can keep records of their radio listening activities for a week's period. Later in the school year, they can repeat the activity and compare the two logs. This provides pupil and teacher with an evaluation of the student's growth in taste and appreciation.

• You can allow pupils to keep their own records of improvement in interpreting directions, in remembering orally presented items, and in remembering facts given in a talk.

DEVELOPING THE ABILITY TO LISTEN

A child's ability to listen attentively should be developed continuously as part of the language arts program and during the study of other disciplines. In line with a social studies unit on communication, for example, you can demonstrate how music is used as a form of communication.

Play recordings of ballads and folk songs about American western heroes. Ask the children to listen carefully to detect events about the lives of these men from the songs. After the recordings are completed, pass out art paper and water colors, and ask children to paint a picture of one of the men, depicting him doing something which they heard in the song.

This technique can be used in any situation where you are attempting to develop listening ability or where students seem to have trouble grasping thoughts by listening. It can be carried a step further by having each student tell his classmates what the picture he has painted shows. Pictures depicting western heroes can then be put into the same sequence as the recordings and placed in a booklet or displayed on the bulletin board.

LEARNING TO LISTEN
THROUGH SELF-EVALUATION

Classroom standards for good listening habits, such as the following, can be established:

1. Look at the person who is speaking.
2. Do not move desks or chairs when someone is speaking.
3. Do not play with things when someone is speaking.
4. Do not interrupt or talk when someone is speaking.
5. Think of questions to ask the speaker while he is speaking, so you can ask them during question time.

Ask each child to prepare his own chart (on oaktag) of these good listening habits. Add a title to the chart, such as "Have I Been a Good Listener?"

After specific lessons designed to foster good listening habits, such as show and tell, oral reports, story time, or recordings, allow pupils time for self-evaluation. Let them refer to their charts. By checking off each item, they can determine for themselves whether they have been good listeners.

This method promotes a conscious effort by children to develop good listening habits. It has an added value of making each pupil consciously take part in a lesson. It is used primarily in grades two through six.

FOSTERING OBSERVATION
AND SEQUENCE SKILLS

Observation, although not specifically a part of the language arts, is important and should be fostered. One way of doing this is to play an early morning game with the children.

When you enter the classroom, touch several objects on the way to your desk. Call on pupils to determine if they remember what you have touched and in what sequence.

TRAINING THE EAR

Much can be done in the vicinity of the school building to train children in listening. For example, supply students with paper and pencil and take them on a "listening walk." Each child lists those things which he hears while walking, such as a bird whistling, a car engine starting, a door closing, and wind rustling in the trees.

When class members return to the room, they can work together in composing a chart. A title for the chart may be, "Our Daily (or weekly) Sound Chart."

Each child relates sounds he has heard and, if his findings are confirmed by another student or you, the sound is recorded on the chart.

If you have a tape recorder, you can record particular sounds. Next day, play the recording for the children and have them decide what made the sounds. This technique can be made into a game by dividing the class into two teams and scoring a point for each correct answer.

These two techniques are suitable for employment on any grade level.

THE USE OF READING TO ENHANCE LISTENING

You can have the children read stories that lend themselves to illustration and sequential discussion. Examples of this type of story are to be found in the book, *Treat Shop,* by Eleanor M. Johnson and Leland B. Jacobs.

The procedure to use for the enhancement of listening ability using the story approach is as follows:

1. Have the class read the story.
2. Discuss the action taking place in the story.
3. List the events occurring in the story on the chalkboard in their proper sequence.
4. Ask for volunteers to draw pictures suggested by the sequence list on the chalkboard.
5. When the pictures are completed, have the class select those that best tell the story for display across the top of the chalkboard or on a bulletin board. Captions should then be written by the children and added to the pictures.

AUDITORY DISCRIMINATION OF SOUNDS

Prepare a list such as the following to check vowel sounds. Other lists may be prepared for testing whether the children can hear beginning consonants, endings and other sounds.

Have the children number their papers for the number of words in the list. After each number, have them write *only* the vowel they hear in the word. Have them show whether it is a long or short vowel by using the symbols $^-$ or $\smile$, respectively.

Your list looks like this:

1.	Went	6.	Yes
2.	Romp	7.	Jig
3.	Hint	8.	Hide
4.	Came	9.	Home
5.	Sleep	10.	Use

The children's papers should look like this:

1.	ĕ	6.	ĕ
2.	ŏ	7.	ĭ
3.	ĭ	8.	ī
4.	ā	9.	ō
5.	ē	10.	ū

FOLLOWING DIRECTIONS

This is a game which utilizes both reading and listening skills. On file cards, write out several simple directions, such as the following:

1. Walk to the door.
2. Tap three times on the door.
3. Hop to your seat.
4. Walk around your chair two times.
5. Sit down.

Directions on each card should differ, and the number of directions and difficulty of words used are determined by the ability of your class to read directions and retain their meanings.

Divide the class into two teams. One team reads all directions off a single card aloud. Directions are read one time only.

A member of the other team must follow the directions exactly as stated. If he follows the directions exactly, he scores a point for his team. If he misses any one of the directions, the point goes to the team which is reading.

Chapter 7. IDEAS TO USE IN TEACHING SOCIAL STUDIES

SUMMARY OF TECHNIQUES

7

IDEAS TO USE IN
TEACHING SOCIAL STUDIES

As you know, social studies is concerned with people and their relationships with other people and with the physical world. This encompasses a great many things, but concerns primarily living in the home and school, living in the neighborhood community, living in the broader community (state and nation), living in different types of world communities, and demonstrating the ability of man to adjust to his environment. The objectives of social studies are to make the child aware of the relationship of man to society and to prepare the child to take his place in society as a good citizen.

Since the study of society is presented by means of the unit approach in most school districts, it is in this way that the ideas in this chapter are offered.

SUMMARY OF ACTIVITIES

There are probably as many methods of teaching social studies in the elementary school as there are teachers. Each educator has her own ideas.

At the outset, then, it is of value to summarize some of the more interesting activities. The remainder of this chapter is devoted to developing these activities to demonstrate how they are employed under varying classroom circumstances.

Activities that can be considered in a social studies program are:

• Use of textbooks, reference books, library books, newspapers, magazines, and other printed materials for research reading.

• Use of resource people for interviews, discussions, and demonstrations.

• Annotation of selected bibliographies.

• Presentation of ideas through pantomime or dramatization.

• Preparation of travel guides for various areas of the world.

• Reading or telling of stories relating to the topic of study.

• Preparation of experience charts.

• Maintaining notebooks and pupil folders as records of activities.

• Visits to museums of science and natural history, and to libraries to view exhibits.

• Presentation of oral reports on topics of study.

• Encouraging pupils to take an active part in such service organizations as the Junior Red Cross and school clubs.

• Exploration of art, music, and folk games to enrich the study of geographical areas.

• Writing of letters to secure pamphlets and other printed information relative to topics of study.

• Preparation of a dictionary of social study words.

• Correspondence by children with children of other countries.

• Making surveys of school and community resources and services.

• Tracing the development of products from raw materials to finished versions and consumption.

• Use of films, television, radio, slides, transparencies, overlays, and recordings to summarize a unit or to extend learning in a particular area of study.

• Preparation of materials for bulletin boards and table displays.

- Maintaining a log of events which occur during a period being studied.
- Planning educational field trips relating to topics of study.
- Preparation of original stories or biographies with countries as a background.
- Holding group discussions to evaluate field trips, situations which can be improved, or projects which have been completed.
- Preparation of a quiz box for use in class.
- Casting of classroom ballots during local, state, or national elections.
- Preparation of exhibits for presentation to other classes.
- Collecting stamps and or coins of countries being studied.
- Holding panel discussions or debates in which children defend different points of view.
- Recreating newspaper stories of a historical period or of a country under study.

CLASSROOM TV

Using a fabricated television or movie set as the basis for teaching a social studies unit is extremely effective. When children are told they will produce a TV show or a movie, interest in the unit is heightened. Sufficient assignments can be made to permit all pupils to take part.

For example, several youngsters can be assigned the task of making the television or movie set. They can use a cardboard carton and two bamboo poles or broom sticks. The front of the carton is cut out. Holes are punched in top and bottom on each side to permit insertion of the poles.

The majority of students can be assigned the job of making the TV or movie script. Each is given a specific picture to draw. For instance, if the unit is concerned with transportation, each child is asked to draw a different picture of a mode of transportation—past, present, or future. The same technique can be applied to any unit of study.

Each student who works on a drawing is also required to write a summary on the bottom of his drawing to describe the illustration. For example, if a child is depicting the invention of the first airplane, he would want to emphasize its inventors, the date of the invention, the impact of the invention, and an interesting or important fact or two about the invention, such as its performance during the first flight.

When all pictures are submitted, the teacher helped by several students, tapes them together in chronological order or in an order that gives cohesion to the presentation. The presentation is then rolled up on one of the bamboo poles or broom sticks, preferably the one on the right as you view the screen. The other end of the presentation is stapled or taped to the other pole. As the left-hand pole is rotated, the film strip unravels across the "screen" from right to left and is taken up on the left-hand spool.

During the lesson, as each frame makes an appearance on the screen, the movement of the strip is stopped and the illustration is discussed.

This idea is best suited for use in the upper elementary grades. If you wish, other classes in the school can be invited to see the "preview." In this way, your class receives training in extending social courtesies to others.

POLITICS IN THE CLASSROOM

Daily classroom activities offer good opportunity for formulation and expression of opinion. Such questions as where to go on a class trip, whether to have a Christmas party or collect money for charity, and what type of playground activities to engage in lead to differences of opinion among class members.

Arriving at a decision should be an orderly and democratic process. Having children form opinion groups to campaign for a "cause," and holding elections emphasize the conduct of politics and good citizenship.

Students who find they hold the same or similar opinions can form a party, hold a convention to nominate candidates for office, draw up a platform, and have candidates and platform voted upon. Candidates can make speeches to sway other class members. Naturally, more than one "political party" is needed to make the technique effective.

At the end of a campaign, an election can be held and voters may cast ballots. An election board complete with "challengers" from each party can be formed to make sure voting is conducted in an orderly manner, and there is no "ballot box stuffing."

The election board counts the ballots and makes the results known.

LEARNING ABOUT COMMUNITY HELPERS

A respect for and appreciation of people who hold jobs concerned with community safety, welfare, and health can be nurtured in youngsters from grade two onward. This idea, which is just one way to accomplish the goal, can be introduced during a unit of study concerned with the community.

Divide the class into several groups. Assign each group the task of making a pictorial chart depicting the work of a community "helper." The chart should emphasize how a community "helper" serves us. The "helpers" selected can be policemen, mailmen, firemen, the mayor, visiting nurses, doctors, milkmen, school teachers, and the like.

Pictures showing the work performed by each "helper" can be clipped from magazines and pasted on the chart. Pictures may also be drawn.

When the assignment is completed, have each group display the chart and explain to the class the function of, need for, and services performed by the "helpers." All charts can be bound together in booklet form.

HOW TO MAKE "HELPERS" COME ALIVE

Another method to present community "helpers" is to have groups of students partake in a community construction project. Set aside a table and assign each group the task of portraying a "helper" in relation to his surroundings.

For example, policemen can be shown near a police station, firemen near a firehouse, doctors and nurses near a hospital, milkmen near a dairy, and so forth. All constructed items can be placed on the table to form a model community.

Characters can be small dolls made from clothespins and

dressed in appropriate uniforms made from fabric scraps, crepe paper, or tissue paper. Paper dolls from cut-out books can also be used. Buildings can be made from shoe boxes covered with construction or wrapping paper.

FLAG WAVING

The flags of states and nations often contain symbols of historical significance. This project for students in grades four to six can serve to acquaint them with the formation of a particular geographic entity or some important historical event.

Assign each child the task of making a flag of a state or country. He should prepare an oral report of how the flag came into existence. When flag and report are complete, he presents both to the class.

Flags can be made any size, but should be kept the shape of the actual flag, usually rectangular. If you desire to have small flags for bulletin board display, they can measure approximately 4" x 2½" or 5" x 3".

A ROOM FULL OF INDIANS

This combination exercise develops good citizenship habits in youngsters (grades two to four), while promoting interest in the study of American Indian heritage.

Have each child make a war bonnet. Oaktag, felt, or a strip of solid-colored fabric can be used for the headband. Allow children to add Indian symbols to bands using paint, crayon, or melted wax.

In employing melted wax, regular crayon pieces are used. The tip is held to a flame for a few seconds and then is quickly applied to the band.

Feathers for the bonnet are cut from oaktag. However, the children should not be permitted to attach feathers to their bonnets. Explain to pupils that feathers for a bonnet were awarded for good deeds in Indian society. A similar approach to earning feathers will be conducted in the classroom.

Discuss the rules of good classroom and school citizenship.

Thereafter, at the end of each school day, ask children to evaluate their individual citizenship for the day. If no rules were broken, a child may place a check mark on a chart which you have prepared listing pupils' names.

If a child has forgotten that he broke a rule, remind him. "I don't believe you deserve a check mark today, Jim," you can say. "Don't you remember that you punched Herman?"

When a child has accumulated four check marks, which do not have to be obtained on consecutive days, place a star on the chart by his name. With the awarding of a star, the pupil is given a feather for his war bonnet. He can color or paint the feather and staple it to his bonnet.

When a child completes his war bonnet, allow him to select an Indian name from a prepared list. This name (and the pupil's real name) is placed on another chart. For example, Chief Red Feather (Jim Smith); Princess Moonbeam (Mary Hill).

The citizenship chart may be continued after the Indian unit is completed. If you don't wish to continue the war bonnet theme, the citizenship chart can be used to form the basis for an honor roll. At the end of a specific period (four weeks, for example), the names of those children who have been awarded the most stars are listed on an honor roll chart.

POTTERY MAKING

Children in grades two to four enjoy making Indian pottery. At the same time, the activity contributes to an understanding of Indian culture.

To make pottery, use powdered clay and water. Powdered clay that dries without baking is now available.

Allow children to make a piece of pottery, such as a dish, bowl, or ashtray. The coil method of molding is easiest for youngsters to negotiate. When the mold dries, children can apply Indian symbols with paint, preferably Testor enamel which is available at hobby shops. Symbols can be placed in the center of the mold and around the outer edge.

To make painting as neat as possible, the following ideas can be employed:

1. To prevent paint bottles from tipping over, fill the tops of coffee cans with Plasticine. Press bottles into the Plasticine.

2. Show pupils how to stir paint, using a toothpick as the mixing tool. Equip each paint bottle with a toothpick.

3. Place turpentine and paper towels in a suitable location. Demonstrate how brushes and hands can be cleaned.

In using Testor enamel, each color must be allowed to dry before a new color is introduced into the mold. Complete drying is essential to prevent colors from running together.

When painting is completed and enamel has dried, coat the mold with clear shellac. Allow to dry and follow with a second coating of shellac. The shellac adds strength, body, and water-proofing to the mold.

JIGSAW PUZZLES

Homemade jigsaw puzzles are useful in supplementing a social studies unit on any grade level. Each puzzle should have a theme, such as a map of a country, a drawing or photograph of a famous person or of an important event. Puzzles can be made increasingly difficult as grade level increases.

Subject material is available from texts, magazines, work-books, and periodicals. The illustration is cut from the book and pasted on heavy cardboard or a piece of thin wood. A coat of shellac is applied to the surface and allowed to dry, after which the mounted picture is cut into small jigsaw pieces.

If cardboard has been used as the puzzle's base, a sharp pair of scissors or a knife is used to make cut-outs. If wood forms the base, a small coping saw or jigsaw can be employed.

TOM-TOM

An interesting Indian crafts project to employ in grades two to four is the making of tom-toms. Coffee cans which have tops and bottoms removed form the cylindrical part of the instrument. Rubber circles for the top and bottom faces can be cut from an old inner tube, if available. Heavy wrapping paper covered with two or three coats of shellac can also be used.

If wrapping paper is employed for the faces, use rubber bands to attach the lower part of the drum to the upper. If inner tube rubber is employed, punch several holes around the edges and use heavy cord to lace the top face to the bottom.

Paint and decorate tom-toms with Indian symbols. A single symbol can be drawn or painted on the top face of the drum.

MAP IDEAS

1. Using outline maps of the geographical area under study, have children show the products representative of the area. They can cut out pictures of these products from magazines or old texts and paste them on the map. They can also draw in products.

2. Using an outline map, make a relief presentation of a state or country. Relief images can be formed from a mixture of flour, salt, and water. Form the mixture into shapes for river beds, mountains, lakes, and plains. When the relief material has dried, areas can be painted with different colors to represent different features. For example, green can represent flat plains, blue can be used to represent water, and brown to represent mountains and highlands.

If this technique is used in lower grades, you will probably have to make the relief map. In higher grades, children can make their own.

GETTING TO KNOW THE COMMUNITY

This exercise serves a dual purpose for pupils in grades one to three: (1) it permits them to learn about community landmarks, such as firehouses, police stations, and town halls; (2) it permits them to become acquainted with the area around the school.

A large sheet of wrapping paper is tacked to the bulletin board. An X or photograph of a school is attached to represent the location of the school building. Children cut out and paste up pictures of various buildings to represent other structures around town. These are placed in proper relationship to the school building. Roads are drawn in.

OVERHEAD PROJECTION FOR MAP STUDIES

If available, an overhead projector can be used for map studies at any grade level in the elementary school. A base transparency is made by reproducing an outline map of a country or section of a country on to a transparent projection material. For example, if the unit of study deals with the southern portion of the United States, reproduce a map showing North Carolina, South Carolina, Georgia, Florida, Tennessee, Alabama, Mississippi, Louisiana, Arkansas, Oklahoma, and Texas. Make sure boundaries are clearly defined.

Make additional transparencies to serve as overlays. These will be placed atop the basic transparency and can show capitals, major cities, mountain ranges, industrial centers, land elevations, and anything else you might like to include. Make as many as needed. These areas can be colored with crayon or grease pencil by applying color directly to transparency material.

Make sure areas represented on overlays are in correct registration to states represented by the basic transparency. All areas you wish to emphasize should fall in their exact locations.

TALKS BY LOCAL OFFICIALS

As part of a program to promote good citizenship in upper elementary students and to aid their understanding of the community, invite local officials into the classroom to speak of their responsibility to the community. Generally, these people are eager to cooperate.

Talks stimulate pupil interest in the town, and give them insight into roles played by public officials. Pupils soon realize they will have the responsibility of citizenship to insure that qualified people are put into positions of public trust.

Officials that can be invited include police, firemen, public librarian, postmaster, visiting nurse, county agricultural agent, township committeeman or mayor, sanitary engineer, and magistrate.

Officials of industrial plants are also usually happy when asked to address classes about their companies and their role in the community. It is often advantageous to exchange visits. Have an official visit the class to explain his company and its work. Then, have the class visit the company to observe.

ANOTHER COMMUNITY IDEA

Obtain photographs of industrial and public buildings in the area. Introduce the buildings to students by discussing what goes on inside. A guest speaker proves most effective. Pictures can also serve as a basis for a bulletin board display entitled, "This Is Your Community."

The idea is suitable on any grade level.

MEETING THE POST OFFICE

To familiarize second to fourth grade pupils with the post office, discuss the postal function and arrange a trip to the local facility. As a supplementary exercise, let each pupil prepare an address book in which he writes the names and addresses of classmates as they would appear on a letter envelope.

GETTING THE MOST FROM A SOCIAL STUDIES UNIT ON COMMUNICATION

Give children experience in developing communications media. Use of the historical approach provides an additional learning experience.

To begin, discuss the history of communications, using texts. As each form is introduced, allow children to participate in an activity that deals with the use and development of the medium.

The following are examples:

a. When the subject of picture writing and pictograms is introduced, discuss how symbols were used instead of words to convey messages. Give each child a strip of paper and ask him to write a one sentence message using picture writing. Have students exchange papers to try to decipher messages.

b. When discussing the history of printing and how early type was made from wood blocks, children can make their own "type" by potato printing.

c. In discussing code, specifically Morse code, explain the function and use of code. Allow children to devise simple coding systems, such as substituting numbers for letters. Allow groups to send messages to each other.

d. During a discussion of newspapers, allow children to discover the different kinds of information a paper has to offer—advertisements, birth announcements, television and radio listings, cartoons, news, sports, and the like. Form the children into groups, giving each the responsibility of gathering information and writing stories about different school happenings. Reports can be prepared, for instance, on upcoming assembly programs, pupils who are ill, administrative announcements, and upcoming sports events. Staple these together in newspaper fashion.

e. In introducing the subject of television as a form of communication, allow children to compose their own TV show as discussed earlier.

As a concluding activity, prepare a list of all communication media that have been discussed. Let each child select one and make a shadow box depicting some phase of its historical development. Shadow boxes can be put on display.

SPORTS AND GEOGRAPHY

Use sports in grades four to six to develop in children a knowledge of geographical names and locations, as follows:

a. Baseball. One corner of the room is home base. Going counterclockwise, the other corners are first base, second base, and third base. Hang a map of a country, state, or continen near home base, and divide the class into Teams A and B. You serve as "pitcher" and scorekeeper.

Team A goes to bat. The first member comes to home base and you say, "Locate St. Louis." If the pupil succeeds within ten seconds, he goes to first base. If he does not, call him out and the next player comes up.

Team A remains at bat, advancing a base each time a correct answer is given, until three players are called out. Then, team B takes its turn. The team with the highest score at the end of the game is the winner.

b. Racing. Each class member is supplied with a copy of the same map. Maps are available from a number of sources, including gasoline stations, chambers of commerce, travel bureaus, and embassies of foreign nations.

Divide the class into two or more teams. Call out a location. The first player to find the location on his map scores a point for his team. The first team to score ten points is the winner.

MAKING BOOKLETS

Students can make illustrated booklets for any social studies unit. For example, if the state of New Jersey is under study, reports and illustrations for the booklets can deal with products, land formations, officials, major cities, history, and major industries.

The same technique can apply to any unit in history. If, for instance, the Pilgrims are being studied, a booklet can include reports of famous Pilgrims, why the Pilgrims decided to come to the New World, their trials and tribulations, their relations with the Indians, and related topics.

In preparing booklets, the class can be divided into groups, with each group assigned a topic. One group should also be assigned the task of designing an illustrated cover.

MATCHING UP MATCHSTICKS

Ignited safety matches can be used in social study construction projects. For example, in constructing a sandtable village, they can be used for making fences, cabins, stockades, and railroads.

To make a fence, fasten the sticks together at regular intervals with thread. Use two rows of thread, one near the top and one near the bottom, to hold sticks in place. Tie the thread to the sticks as you proceed.

SOCIAL STUDY UNIT CONSIDERATIONS
FOR LOWER GRADES

The scope of the social studies program in the lower elementary grades is usually influenced by the facilities of school and community. Activities should contribute to an understanding of important phases of social life with which the student comes into contact at home, in the community, and in other social situations. The following examples will explain:

a. Communication and transportation. Activities should serve to foster understanding of transportation and communication. Even children of pre-school age have an awareness of the importance these play in life. They see the telephone used. They watch television. They see people reading newspapers. They see cars, trucks, airplanes, and trains. This veritable wonderland of inventions should be brought into focus in the school. Children should be made to relate themselves to communication and transportation media. This area of the social studies program could be interrelated with the science phase of the curriculum.

b. Consumption of goods and services. Activities should permit children to develop habits of proper selection and use of materials. It should also give them an appreciation for those who provide services on local, state, and national levels.

c. Protection of life and property. This area can be a transition period for a child from an individual to a socialized human being. It should instill in him an awareness of the rights of others and lay stress on individual and group responsibility in society.

d. Recreation. The school can be responsible for developing in children an enduring interest and skill in wholesome recreation. Social studies units should include provision for broadening and developing individual as well as group abilities for recreative enterprises.

e. Work. The social significance of work and the interdependence of workers are concepts that should be developed from the beginning.

Although these phases of social life overlap, you will find it expedient to think in terms of separate topics when selecting activities. No one unit or series of units can exhaust possibilities for treatment. Each is of fundamental importance in curriculum planning because all activities should be selected, planned and evaluated partly in terms of the contribution they make to the child's ability to participate in such essential phases of life.

The chart in Figure 7-1 demonstrates how one unit in each of the three lower elementary grades transcends these phases. It is offered as a guide in planning your units.

PLANNING UNIT SEQUENCES

Two problems of sequence arise when planning a social studies unit. The first is planning a sequence of experiences within one grade level.

Experience leads to experience, and interest to interest. Experience and interest are individual matters affected by diverse factors, such as the child's ability, background, and environment. In planning social studies units, you have to decide which of the many steps open to you are in keeping with the needs of the group and the possibilities of the teaching situation.

The second problem is to plan the sequence from one grade level to the next. Some units are more appropriate in one grade than another. Some concepts are more difficult than others, and interests and capabilities will become more mature with each succeeding grade level.

In estimating the possibilities of unit development, you will find it useful to ask yourself the following questions:

• Does the unit suggest a number of worthwhile problems on the level of understanding?

INTERRELATIONSHIP OF INSTRUCTIONAL OBJECTIVES

Grade	Unit	Transportation; Communication	Consumption of Goods	Life; Property	Recreation	Work
1	"We Go to School"	How we get to school How we go from room to room How rooms are connected by intercom with the office How we write letters How we share ideas	How the milkman gets his milk How we use milk How the grocer serves us How the lunchroom serves us How we get ready for our party How we use supplies	How the policeman helps to keep us safe How the safety guards help us How the engineer keeps us warm How the custodian keeps the building clean How we share in the maintenance of the school building How the nurse and doctor help us How we improve the general health of the school by keeping well ourselves	How we play in the classroom; in the playground How we participate in room projects How we participate in school-wide projects How we enjoy a show How we enjoy the school library	How we work in school How each helper works for all of us How we aid school helpers How tools are used How machinery works
2	"The Librarian"	How books can be a means of sharing the ideas of other people	Where we can go to get books to read	What rules we should follow in using the library	How we can enjoy books during our leisure hours	What the librarian does to keep books in order

Grade	Unit	Transportation; Communication	Consumption of Goods	Life; Property	Recreation	Work
2 (cont.)	"The Librarian"	How the library provides books for us when we live far from the branch; how the book wagon serves people	Where we can find the nearest branch library What part of the library is set off for the kind of books we read How we can renew books when we have not finished reading them How the librarian helps us to use the library How we can help the librarian	How we can help care for books	How books can help us find out more about our hobbies	What helpers the librarian has What work the librarian does when we bring books back; when we renew books What the librarian does to keep the library attractive
3	"The American Indian"	What means of transportation the Indian used How the Indians conveyed messages	How the Indians made their clothes from natural materials How the Indians obtained food from natural resources How the Indians traded with the white men	How the Indians protected themselves from their enemies	What sports the Indians enjoyed	How the Indians divided work among men and women How the Indian men hunted, fished, planted How the Indian women cooked How the Indian built his home

Figure 7-1.

111

• Will it broaden the social outlook of pupils by giving them actual and vicarious contacts with important phases of social life?

• Will it provide opportunities for development of desirable personality traits, such as initiative, perseverance, cooperation, and tolerance?

• Will it provide a number of individual and group activities that will clarify concepts?

• Does it provide valuable information as well as broad understanding?

• Are there sufficient materials available to make it worthwhile?

IDEAS TO USE
FOR A TRANSPORTATION UNIT

Class interest can be stimulated by playing recordings of different modes of transportation. Ideally, this should be done when the unit is first introduced.

As each mode of transportation is discussed, use an art form (reproduction of paintings, photographs, music) to impress that famous artists hold transportation in high esteem as a necessity of modern life. For example, when discussing travel by water, display reproductions of famous paintings that show different types of ships under various circumstances. These can be arranged on the bulletin board under the heading, "Many Famous Artists Painted Pictures of Ships."

Safety, especially in the car, should be an important phase of a unit on transportation. After listing safety factors that should prevail when riding in an automobile, introduce children to games they can play while riding in a car. Stress that games are fun and help to maintain safety standards.

Allow children to play a few of these games in class. The following are examples:

    1. One child states, "I am going to _____ (name of a place). I will buy _____ (start with letter *a*)."
Suppose the child states he will buy an apple.
    The second child also says, "I am going to _____. I

will buy _____ (repeat the item mentioned by the first child and add an item beginning with the letter *b*)." For example, banana.

The children take turns. The object of the game is to see how far each child can go, remembering and repeating in order what has been mentioned, and adding an item starting with the next letter of the alphabet.

2. Travel bingo can be played in the car. Demonstrate how to construct travel bingo cards. The card is a square divided into blocks. Each block contains a drawing of something children would see along the road. As the children ride along, they mark off each of the items they spot. The child who fills his card first is the winner.

When the transportation unit is completed, have children construct a "travel city." A piece of large board (plywood, hardboard, or wallboard) is used. Transportation facilities (railroad station, airport, bus depot, truck terminal) are put in. The board is painted. Masking tape is used for roads and airplane runways. Matchsticks are used for making railroad tracks. Construction paper can be used to make other items. Paste pipe cleaners to constructed parts to serve as stands for mounting.

Children can bring to school model figures and transportation items for the city. These items should emphasize modes of transportation, such as cars, trucks, airplanes, railroad cars, bicycles, and scooters.

USE OF THE SANDTABLE IN THE SOCIAL STUDIES PROGRAM

Reconstructing a community by means of a sandtable promotes in students an understanding of people and their way of life. You can reconstruct practically anything, past or present, with accessories for the table being made of construction paper, Plasticine or plastic figures.

Reconstruction of scenes is a valuable teaching aid on any elementary grade level. However, pupils—not you—should be responsible for projects.

The following are descriptions of scenes you will find interesting:

a. A Village of the Plains Indians. Use oaktag or construction paper to make tepees. Cut out a large circle. Cut a smaller circle in the center of the large circle. Form the circle into a cone shape, and paste or staple together. The appearance will be that of a tepee.

Add decorations. Note that the small hole at the top of the tepee represents a smoke vent. Toothpicks can be pasted around the hole's edge so they extend through the hole to represent the braces Indians used for their shelters.

The remainder of the village can contain a body of water (represented by blue construction paper), small plastic Indian figures, and dogs and horses which can be purchased or made of clay.

b. Eskimo Village. Igloos can be made from one-half of a rubber ball. Cover with papier-mâché or white construction paper. Paste a piece of oaktag fashioned into an oblong shape to the ball to represent the tunnel into the igloo. Paint with white tempera paint for a brilliant finish. Finally, draw in horizontal and vertical black lines with black paint or a felt marker to give the structure the appearance of having been made from blocks of ice.

The Eskimo village scene should also have Eskimo figures and animals (dogs, seals, polar bears) that can be purchased or made of Plasticine or clay. Accessories such as sleighs can be made from construction paper or clay.

ADDITIONAL IDEAS
WITH THE OVERHEAD PROJECTOR

If teaching U. S. history to an upper elementary grade, a topic for discussion may be, "How did the United States grow?" An overhead projector can be used effectively to illustrate this graphically.

Reproduce an outline map of the United States onto a sheet of transparent overhead-projection material. Color in east and west boundaries, represented by the Atlantic and Pacific, with a blue felt marker.

Use a different colored felt marker to color in land areas as you discuss growth of the country. The students will be able to see the development.

You can do coloring as follows:

- The original area of the United States to the Mississippi River: color in light green.
- Louisiana Purchase: color in dark green.
- The territory ceded by Great Britain in 1818 when the 49th parallel was established as the boundary between Canada and the United States: color in red.
- Florida Purchase: color in orange.
- Texas Annexation: color in yellow.
- Mexican Cession: color in purple.
- Gadsen Purchase: color in blue.
- Oregon territory: color in orange.
- Alaskan and Hawaiian acquisitions: color in brown.

You can also use overhead projection for defining terms. For example, suppose your class is learning the terms peninsula, bay, gulf, isthmus, delta, atoll, lowland, plain, and the like.

Make a free-hand drawing of a peninsula and reproduce it on a sheet of transparent overhead-projection material. Make an overlay that contains terms. When you put the overlay on top of the free-hand drawing, the terms should fall over the area to which they apply.

When drawing and overlay are projected simultaneously, students can see what the terms refer to.

After terms have been learned, remove the overlay and place a clear sheet of unexposed transparency material over the drawing. Lay a grease pencil on the projector and divide the class into teams to play, "I know a place which is _____ ."

The captain of team A asks a member of team B, "I know a place which is a gulf. Do you?"

The student being asked goes to the projector and writes in "gulf." If correct, his team gets a point. If in error, a member of team A can correct the error and score a point for his team.

Terms can be better understood by lower grade pupils if an overhead projector is used to show pictures to which terms apply. Keep in mind that you can reproduce a colored picture from a magazine by use of color lift transparent film. This enables you to project full-colored pictures of deserts, polar regions, jungles, mountains, valleys and so forth.

Chapter 8. TEACHING ARITHMETIC THROUGH ACTIVITY

SUMMARY OF TECHNIQUES

117

8

TEACHING
ARITHMETIC THROUGH ACTIVITY

Numbers become significant and meaningful to a child through contact with the quantitative aspects of daily living. The teaching of arithmetic, therefore, calls for a planned program that builds fundamental skills. For the program to be of maximum value, the teacher should vitalize and make effective this systematic instruction by capitalizing upon every opportunity to apply learning to the problems that students meet in their everyday lives.

The activities discussed in this chapter will permit you to add meaning and interest to your arithmetic program. It should be kept in mind that each activity must be viewed in relation to the objective which you are trying to accomplish.

The objectives of an arithmetic program in the elementary grades are as follows:

• To develop an awareness of the usefulness of numbers in everyday life.

• To develop the ability to meet situations which arise in connection with classroom activities.

- To stimulate a permanent interest in number processes.
- To promote self-reliance in discovering quantitative relationships in natural situations.
- To develop concepts of time in connection with the activities in the home and school.
- To provide and use every available opportunity for developing understanding and appreciation of money values.
- To provide a variety of activities in which simple measurements will be needed.
- To develop a meaningful number vocabulary and a background of number concepts through school activities.
- To encourage and provide opportunities for writing numbers in classroom situations.
- To develop fundamental personal and social habits, such as economy, fair play, sharing, good judgment and cooperation.

LET'S GO FISHING

This game can be used in place of drillwork in the primary grades. It will accomplish the same purposes, but in a more interesting manner.

The object of the game is to teach basic number facts. Fashion many small fishes, but have two groups, each of one color—red and blue, for example. Make them of poster board. Write a number fact on each, and place a metal staple at the mouth of each.

Make two fishing poles from dowel sticks or toy drumsticks. Tie a string to each and place a small magnet on the end of each string. Also needed are two plastic or wooden containers, one marked with a piece of red poster paper and the other with blue, each holding only fish of the same color. A large box divided into ten parts numbered consecutively from one to ten is also required.

Divide the class into two teams: red and blue. On signal from you, a student from each team approaches his respective colored container and fishes. When he catches one, he determines the answer of the number facts and drops the fish into a section of the large box he believes corresponds to the answer. The student returns to his team and passes the fishing pole to the next child.

The team which finishes first is awarded five points. Answers are checked by having each team check the other's answers. A point is awarded for each correct answer, and a point is deducted for each incorrect answer.

A CARD GAME FOR SMALL GROUPS

This game can be a substitute for small-group individual drill-work. It is played by four, five, or six pupils.

At least 40 cards are needed, but keep in mind that the exact number should be equally divisible by the number of players. For example, if there are five players, use 45 or 50 cards.

Divide cards into equal groups and write problems on them, making sure the problems in each group are of the same kind. For example, if you have 40 cards, use ten cards for addition problems, ten for subtraction, ten for multiplication, and ten for division.

Each type of problem should be written in a different color. For instance, addition problems can be written in green, subtraction problems in red, multiplication problems in blue, and division problems in black.

A player shuffles and deals the cards. The player on the dealer's left starts the game by playing any card he wishes to the center of the table. As he plays the card, he calls out the answer to the problem on the card.

The play passes to the left, with each pupil playing a card of the *same* color and announcing his answer. The object is to play a card which has a higher answer than the one played previously.

When each player has played a round, the one who has the highest answer takes the trick and leads another card of his choice.

If a player cannot play the same colored card that is being led, he passes. Players should be on guard to make sure that announced answers are correct.

The first player to play off all his cards wins the game, but play should continue until all but one have no cards left.

This game can be introduced on lower grade levels, but can also be used in higher grades by devising advanced problems for use on cards.

THE SPINNING WHEEL

Make a spinning wheel 12 to 18 inches in diameter, using oaktag. Write numbers from zero through nine around the perimeter. Devise a one-inch wide pointer from oaktag and attach to the wheel by placing a metal washer between the wheel and pointer. Then, push a paper fastener through the pointer into the wheel.

You will need several one-inch square cards. Write a numeral from one through nine on each. The cards are attached, one at a time, to the pointer with a paper clip. This is the base fact.

To use, spin the pointer. The number at which it stops is added or multiplied to the base fact.

The value of the spinning wheel is primarily as a drilling tool in addition and multiplication. Generate more interest by dividing the class into teams for a game. Each child spins the pointer and has five seconds in which to give a correct answer to score a point for his team.

YOU'RE IT

A game of arithmetic tag to provide second to fourth grade pupils with fundamental drillwork can be played if there is sufficient room.

Form pupils into a circle. To begin the game, ask two or three students to act as members of the "scrub team." They enter the center of the circle. Another student is asked to be "it."

The one who is "it" skips or walks around the outside of the circle and stops in back of a student. Tapping him on the shoulder, he presents a problem, such as "three plus four is how many?" or "six from ten is how much?" or "four times three is how many?"

The challenged player must call out the correct answer before someone on the scrub team. If he does, he becomes "it." If he doesn't he exchanges places with the member of the scrub team who gave the correct answer.

You act as umpire.

RING-TOSS GAME

This game is used in grades two to four to provide students with drill in addition, subtraction, multiplication, and division.

Mark off a large square on the floor in chalk and divide it into nine equal parts. Write a number from one through nine in each part. The square can also be marked off on cardboard or oaktag and fastened to the floor with masking tape.

A bean bag or clean eraser is used for the tossing device. It is thrown at the square from a distance of six to eight feet.

To use the ring-toss for addition, two or more tosses are made by a pupil who must give the sum of the numbers on which the tossing device falls. Or you can call out a number and have the student make one toss to obtain another number for addition.

In doing subtraction, give a number. One toss is made to get a number to subtract from it.

For multiplication, two tosses are made to get two numbers to multiply. Or, again, you can call out a number, and the student need make only one toss.

To use the device for division, give a number to be divided by the number obtained from a toss. If it is not desirable to have remainders, cover over those numbers that aren't needed.

NUMBER AIDS

To help lower grade children to understand number concepts, keep several objects on hand, such as pebbles, toothpicks, used kitchen matches, or acorns. When a pupil has trouble in understanding an addition or subtraction concept, allow him to formulate the problem by using the objects.

TIC-TAC-TOE, ARITHMETIC STYLE

Draw a tic-tac-toe box on the blackboard. Write a word description of a problem in each box.

For example, problems that apply to a fifth or sixth grade arithmetic class are multiplication, symbols, addition of fractions, famous mathematicians, decimals, multiplication of fractions, important formulas, computation, and percentages. Have problems for each category prepared to present to students.

Divide the class into two teams and give each a symbol, such as X and O. Flip a coin to determine which team starts, and a player selects the topic he wishes to try by stating the description given in the box. Present the problem.

If the player gives the correct answer, write the team symbol in the square. If the student fails to answer the question, no symbol is given. Play passes to the other team.

The object of the game is to get three of the same symbols in a straight line: in a row, column, or diagonal line. Teams will have to be careful to select problems that block their opponents.

The game is suited for use in grades five and six, but the same technique can be used in lower grades for number fact drillwork.

MORE TIC-TAC-TOE

This technique is an individual exercise in adding numbers mentally. It is suitable for use in the upper elementary grades.

One player is assigned odd numbers—one, three, five, seven, and nine. The other player uses even numbers— two, four, six, and eight. The player with the odd numbers begins the game by writing a number into a square of a conventional tic-tac-toe box.

The object of the game is to get numbers in a row (down, across, or diagonally) that add up to 15. Players alternate placement of numbers into squares. They cannot use a number more than once.

The following are examples:

7	6	1
5	8	4
3	2	9

Figure 8-1.

Order of play: 7, 6, 1, 4, 9, 2, 3, 8, 5.
Winner: Odd number player with 7, 5, 3.

8	5	2
4		9
		7

Figure 8-2.

Order of play: 5, 4, 7, 2, 9, 8.
Winner: Even number player with 8, 5, 2.

3	7	1
5	9	8
6	2	4

Figure 8-3.

Order of play: 7, 2, 9, 8, 3, 4, 1, 6, 5.
The game is a draw.

YOUNG PERSON'S BINGO

Use this game in the first and second grades to foster number recognition. Prepare bingo cards that consist of four horizontal rows of five numbers. Make sure there are no vertical rows of four numbers on the card, which might confuse youngsters. An example of a card for this game is Figure 8-4.

3		6		13		19		10
	8	12			11		7	5
	4		2	16		14	17	
1		9	15		18			20

Figure 8-4.

The object of the game is to cover all numbers in a horizontal row. Call numbers from prepared slips of paper markers. It would be best on this grade level for numbers not to exceed 20.

The first student to cover five numbers in a row calls "Bingo."

BINGO FOR GRADES THREE AND FOUR

A bingo game for third and fourth grade students provides drill in simple problems. Prepare bingo cards that offer problems in addition, subtraction, multiplication, and division which are answerable in numbers from one to 20. The last row of the card is left blank for answers. A sample card is shown in Figure 8-5.

16	12	3	10	19
÷4	+7	X5	÷2	−11

Figure 8-5.

To play the game, pull slips from a box and call out numbers written on them. If a number is an answer to a problem on his card, the student writes the answer in the square below the problem.

The first player to fill in all blank squares calls "Bingo."

FOOTBALL

Number football is an interesting method to use for addition and multiplication drillwork. Divide the class into two teams, and select a quarterback for each group.

Draw a diagram of a football field on the blackboard. (See Figure 8-6.) Mark off each ten yards with a number as seen in the example below. Draw in a football. The quarterback of the defensive team writes a number in the football.

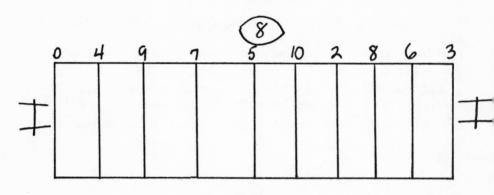

Figure 8-6.

The quarterback of the offensive team calls on a team member to carry the ball by adding or multiplying each ten-yard number by the number written in the football. If he carries the ball the length of the field without a mistake he scores a touchdown for his team. If he makes a mistake or hesitates too long, the defensive team calls "down" and another player is called upon to carry the ball.

If a team fails to score in four downs, the opposing group takes the ball on whatever yard marker it is on. The opposite team quarterback now writes in a number of his choice, and the game proceeds with the ball-carrying team heading toward the other team's goal.

BASEBALL

Baseball fans can play their game to develop number concepts. Divide the class into two teams and appoint a pitcher for each.

Draw a diagram of a baseball diamond on the blackboard and place a number at each of the four bases. The pitcher of the team in the field writes a number in the pitcher's box.

The player at bat must give the sum, difference, product, or quotient of the number in the pitcher's box with those at each of the four bases. If he gets the correct answer at first base, he is awarded a single. He now has the option of taking his single and passing the bat to a team member, or he can try for a double, triple, or home run. However, he must proceed in consecutive order around the bases.

If he gives a wrong answer which is caught by a member of the opposing team, he is out. Any base which he won prior to being called out is automatically relinguished.

The opposing pitcher can change the number in the pitcher's box whenever he wishes after a pupil has batted. During the game, you should change the numbers at each of the four bases as well.

After a team makes three outs, the team in the field gets their chance at bat.

DEVELOPING ARITHMETICAL SKILLS
IN GRADE ONE

Youngsters can acquire basic number concepts and arithmetical skills by relating them to social situations. Many number requirements arise as a social unit is developed, and you should be quick to take advantage of them.

For example, suppose a unit is dealing with a member of the retail trade as, for example, a toy store. This would offer good opportunity to familiarize youngsters with time and money values, number recognition, and simple addition.

The following are several arithmetical possibilities which present themselves:

• Planning a trip to a store by studying the calendar to ascertain a suitable date.

• Estimating the length of time of travel to store from school by bus.

• Ascertaining the time to leave school to catch the bus and the time to return for dismissal.

• Learning hour and half-hour concepts.

• Determining the number of students who will go on the trip.

- Computing the amount of money each will need for bus fare.
- Bringing the bus fare to school and counting the money.
- Determining in the store how much merchandise costs by examining price tags.
- Measuring out space in the classroom for establishment of a sample store.
- Determining the size and number of shelves for merchandise in the in-class store.
- Discussing sizes and shapes of merchandise, which the children can bring from home.
- Estimating prices to charge for in-class store merchandise.
- Making play money.
- Buying and selling items in the in-class store.

SOCIAL ACTIVITIES THAT DEVELOP ARITHMETICAL SKILLS

There are various social situations in and around the school which can be used to develop arithmetical skills, such as the following:

SITUATIONS IN THE LIBRARY

- Using the telephone directory to find the library's phone number and calling to determine its hours of service.
- Estimating the time for walking from school to library.
- Estimating what time the class must leave school to arrive at the library at a given hour.
- Estimating how much time the class can spend at the library.
- Counting the number of children who will make the trip.
- Determining how many book shelves are needed for an in-class library corner.
- Determining the size of in-class book shelves.
- Determining the number of tables and chairs for a reading corner.
- Measuring materials for curtains, chair covers, and table scarfs to decorate the reading corner.

- Determining the number of books for the in-class library.
- Keeping records of children who serve as librarian to give each a turn.

SITUATIONS THAT CAN BE DEVELOPED FROM CLASSROOM PARTIES

- Visiting stores to determine prices of food and decorations.
- Contacting the school milkman to determine the price of milk and ice cream.
- Deciding date and time for the party.
- Determining the length of time required to serve lunch.
- Determining the number of people to be served.
- Measuring servings of milk to estimate the number of quarts that will be needed.
- Reading recipes for cookies, purchasing ingredients, and measuring ingredients.
- Determining how many cookies to make.
- Learning the meanings of dozen, half-dozen, quart, and pint.
- Counting utensils for setups.
- Computing the cost of the party.
- Computing the cost per pupil.

SITUATIONS THAT DEVELOP FROM EVERYDAY CLASS ACTIVITIES

- Counting the number of children in the class.
- Counting the number present and absent.
- Counting the number of children buying lunch.
- Counting the number of books needed for a reading group.
- Reading page numerals in a book.
- Reading page numerals in a table of contents.
- Reading numerals on classroom doors.
- Recognizing house numerals.
- Reading telephone numerals.
- Reading numerals on a scale when children are weighed in the nurse's office.
- Keeping scores of games played in the classroom.

THE MEANING OF EQUATIONS

When equations are introduced, their meanings can be kept before your pupils by preparing a reference card for each child to place in his arithmetic book. The cards can be duplicated on oaktag.

One object is to teach the commutative property. For instance, as regards addition, it should be stressed that no matter how the addends are switched, the answer remains the same ($3 + 2 = 5$; $2 + 3 = 5$).

The following are samples you may wish to use:

COMBINING:

Not Equal Groups—Add:

Number to start	Plus	Number added	Equals	Number in all	Computation
4	+	3	=	7	4 +3 —— 7

Equal Groups—Add:

Number to start	Plus	Number added	Equals	Number in all	Computation
5	+	5	=	10	5 +5 —— 10

Equal Groups—Multiply:

Number of groups	Times	Number in each group	Equals	Number in all	Computation
2	×	3	=	6	3 ×2 —— 6

SEPARATING:

Not Equal Groups—Subtract:

Number in all	Minus	Number taken away	Equals	Number remaining	Computation
7	−	3	=	4	7 −3 —— 4

Equal Groups—Subtract:

Number in all	Minus	Number taken away	Equals	Number remaining	Computation
10	−	5	=	5	$\begin{array}{r} 10 \\ -5 \\ \hline 5 \end{array}$

Equal Groups—Divide:

Number in all	Divided by	Number in each group	Equals	Number of groups	Computation
6	÷	3	=	2	$3\overline{)6}$ with 2

You can point out to the class that in an additive situation the first group does not move and the second group moves over to join the first group. When you multiply, all groups move together. When you subtract, a group moves away from the original group. In dividing, the groups all move away from each other. To further emphasize these principles, you can use the diagrams in Figure 8-7.

Add:	Multiply:	Subtract:	Divide:
00 ← 00 00 ← 00 4 + 4 = □	00 → ← 00 00 → ← 00 2 × 4 = □	00 ⌠ 0 → 0 ⌡ 00 6 − 3 = □	← ⟨000⟩ ⟨000⟩ → 6 ÷ 3 = □

Figure 8-7.

STEPS YOU USE TO SOLVE PROBLEMS:

1. Read the problem carefully.
2. Is the action combining or separating?
3. Does the problem state equal or not equal groups?
4. Determine whether the problem is to add, subtract, multiply or divide.
5. What does the question ask?
6. Write the equation with the unknown in the proper place.
7. Solve the equation, making sure the answer in the computation is put in the correct place in the equation.

ESTIMATING WEIGHTS AND MEASURES

Skill in estimating length, distance, weight, and quantity can be introduced to children in grades five and six.

For example, have pupils at the blackboard draw their concept of length, such as six inches, nine inches, 12 inches, two feet, one yard. Check with a ruler. Other activities are to ask the class to estimate the number of beans in a jar, the number of people in the auditorium, the weight of a book, the height of a classmate, and the room's dimensions. Practice in estimating permits pupils to eventually visualize measurements.

If you wish, make a game of accuracy in estimating, by dividing the class into teams. Let them compete for the highest score.

ARITHMETICAL SHUFFLEBOARD

Make the shuffleboard court from a large calendar showing any month. Mount the sheet on cardboard. One board can serve two to five players.

The object of the game is to toss an object, such as beans, on numbered squares and compute the sum. Distance of players from the court is about six feet. The first player to get a cumulative score of 100 wins.

Allow each player two tosses per turn. The sum of the numbers on which the beans land is the player's score for that turn. The sum is added to the score of the previous turn. Each player should compute his own score. If a bean falls off the court or on a line, the score for that toss is zero.

This game can be used in the third and fourth grades. It can be played quietly in the rear of the room after seatwork activities or during a rainy day recess period.

NUMBER BOWLING

Place ten clothespins of the stand-up type on a table in bowling formation. The player rolls a small rubber ball across the table into the pins.

Another student picks up those pins that are knocked down. The only way the player can determine how many pins he knocked down is to subtract the number standing from ten.

The pupil who rolls the ball should close his eyes when he releases the ball. He opens them when the pins have been picked up. If the player gives the correct answer, he gets a point. The first student to accumulate ten points, wins the game.

This game can be used in grades two and three.

BASIC FACTS CHART

You may wish to have each child prepare a chart of addition, subtraction, multiplication, and division number facts. Columns for an addition number chart, for example, are marked off with numerals from two to 18, with each representing a number group.

When facts for each group have been learned, the child can write them in equation form under the appropriate heading. As the chart fills up, the pupil is able to make several observations concerning various groups, such as the following:

1. The number of facts in any one group as compared to other groups.
2. The reverse order of the numbers added.
3. Each group from two to ten has one less fact in it than the value of the group numeral itself.
4. The diminishing number of facts contained in each group from 11 to 18.

A similar chart may be prepared for basic facts in subtraction, multiplication, and division. Heading for a subtraction chart are the same as for the addition chart. Heading for a mutiplication chart require more space (20 columns). These headings are 4, 6, 8, 9, 10, 12, 14, 15, 16, 18, 20, 21, 24, 25, 27, 28, 30, 32, 35, 36. Headings for the division chart are the same as for the multiplication chart. Pupils in grades two and three benefit from this reference material.

Figure 8-8 is an example of an addition fact chart.

ADDITION NUMBER FACT CHART

2	3	4	5	6	7	8	9	10	11	12	13	14	15	16	17	18
1+1	1+2	3+1	2+3	3+3	6+1	7+1	8+1	9+1	9+2	9+3	9+4	9+5	9+6	9+7	9+8	9+9
	2+1	1+3	3+2	4+2	1+6	1+7	1+8	1+9	2+9	3+9	4+9	5+9	6+9	7+9	8+9	
		2+2	4+1	2+4	5+2	6+2	7+2	8+2	8+3	8+4	8+5	8+6	8+7	8+8		
			1+4	5+1	2+5	2+6	2+7	2+8	3+8	4+8	5+8	6+8	7+8			
				1+5	4+3	5+3	6+3	7+3	7+4	7+5	7+6	7+7				
					3+4	3+5	3+6	3+7	4+7	5+7	6+7					
						4+4	5+4	6+4	6+5	6+6						
							4+5	4+6	5+6							
								5+5								

Figure 8-8.

136

USING THE OVERHEAD PROJECTOR
TO TEACH ARITHMETIC

The overhead projector offers several advantages when used to teach arithmetic, as follows:

• It permits organized sequential development of mathematical principles.

• It saves time. You can, for example, repeat part of a lesson without erasing and rewriting.

• It enables you to vary presentations, drill, and quizzes.

• Materials are always on hand to refer students to data which have been previously presented.

The three techniques that follow demonstrate the value of the overhead projector when used to teach arithmetic.

RULES WE GO BY

Transparencies that emphasize mathematical rules can be prepared for projection. For example, four transparencies, which are outlined below, can be used in the third and fourth grades to teach students basic rules of addition, subtraction, multiplication, and division. Through projection, students can see the relationships and similarities of these rules.

Each transparency should impart a rule in an attractive style. Animation can be combined with text. Keep the transparency simple and uncluttered, and put no more than two rules on it.

Transparency No. 1:

a. If zero is added to a number, the answer is that number.
b. If zero is subtracted from a number, the answer is that number.

Transparency No. 2:

a. The order in which numbers are added does not affect the sum.
b. The order in which factors are multiplied does not affect the product.

Transparency No. 3:

a. The ways in which numbers are grouped does not affect the sum.

b. The ways in which factors are multiplied does not affect the product.

Transparency No. 4:

a. If a number is multiplied by one, the product is that number.

b. If the number is divided by one, the quotient is that number.

TEACHING FRACTIONS
BY OVERHEAD PROJECTION

Fractions can be taught by means of overhead projection. For instance, you can introduce basic fractional concepts using four transparencies.

The first transparency consists of a large square which fills the area. Text in the square's center reads, "Whole or One." This transparency remains in position on the projector throughout the lesson.

The other three transparencies are overlays. They are placed over the first transparency one at a time to demonstrate a concept.

Overlay one consists of a square divided equally by a vertical line. Each of the divisions is marked "1 2," and text outside the square reads, "1 2 + 1 2 = 2 2; 2 2 = 1." When this transparency is placed atop the first transparency on the projector, students can observe that 1 2 + 1 2 = 1.

Overlay two consists of a square divided into three equal parts by vertical lines. Each division is marked "1 3," and text outside the square reads, "1 3 + 1 3 + 1 3 = 3 3; 3 3 = 1." This overlay is employed in the same manner as overlay one.

The final overlay consists of a square divided by horizontal and vertical lines into four equal parts. Each part is marked "1 4," and text outside the square reads, "1/4 + 1 4 + 1/4

+ 1/4 = 4/4; 4/4 = 1." This overlay is used in the same manner as the other two.

Be sure that the lines which comprise the square of the overlays are in perfect registration with the lines that make up the square of the first transparency.

PROJECTING MANIPULATIVE DEVICES

Transparent tools and devices used in arithmetic—straight rulers, triangles, protractors, slide rules, and the like—when placed on the overhead projector will be projected onto the screen. An opaque object placed on the projector will cast its shadow outline onto the screen. This could be important to you in teaching arithmetic.

For example, suppose you are introducing geometric shapes to pupils in grades five and six. You can make a manipulative device from four strips of oaktag and hinge them together with pin clips. Moving the parts by hand permits you to change the object's shape.

If you place the device on the projector, its shadow is cast on the screen. As you manipulate the device to obtain various geometric forms, students can see changes taking place.

Suppose you are teaching students how to tell time. Draw a clock dial on white paper and reproduce it on transparent material. If you wish to add color, you can outline the reproduced clock dial or numbers with a grease pencil.

Make hands for the clock from oaktag or cardboard, punch a hole in the center of the dial, and attach the hands to the clock with a pin clip. This allows movement of the hands.

Place the presentation on the projector. Because it is transparent, the clock face and numbers are projected. Because the clock hands are opaque, they are projected as shadow outlines.

SPIN IT

This method is one for full class participation. Although described here to illustrate basic facts of the 14 group, the same idea is applicable to other groups and for mixed facts of any group.

Cut out a six inch square from oaktag. Draw a circle, but leave sufficient margin between the circle's rim and the edge of the oaktag so children can hold the card without covering the circle.

Divide the circle into 12 equal parts. Make a firm pencil or crayon line to delineate each part.

Fasten a paper clip to the center of the circle by pushing the flanges of a pin clip through the paper clip and the center of the circle. Fasten the brad loosely to allow the paper clip to spin.

Have students write an equation for the number group into each divided section. For the 14 group, equations that can be used are $7 + 7 = $; $5 + 9 = $; $9 + 5 = $; $8 + 6 = $; $6 + 8 = $; $2 \times 7 = $; $7 \times 2 = $; $14 \div 2 = $; $14 \div 7 = $; $14 - 7 = $; $14 - 9 = $; $14 - 8 = $.

Allow each child a turn at spinning the wheel. He reads the basic fact aloud. If the clip stops on a line, he spins again.

All children then write the problem in equation form and the answer in a column. The wheel passes from child to child.

STUMP THE PANEL

A panel of three to six students is selected, and the remainder of the class is divided into two teams. Each team composes a set of questions, problems, or terms to ask panel members. Questions should be those which can be answered without written computation. The type of questions depends upon grade level.

For example, several sample questions which can be asked of students in grades five and six are:

1. What number is an even divisor of all whole numbers?
2. How much is 1 4 + 3 8?
3. How many tens are there in 8732?
4. What percentage of 4 is 8?
5. Give an example of digit, ratio, integer, perfect number, general number, improper fraction.
6. Who wrote the most famous geometry book?
7. What is the formula for the area of a circle?
8. Describe an octagon.

Members of each team take turns asking questions. If the panel, working together, answers a question correctly, the panel gets a point. If the panel cannot answer, but a member of the opposing team does, that team gets the point. If neither can answer, the asking team gets a point.

ʃOME DRILLING METHODS

There are many ways of conducting arithmetic drill on the primary grade level. The following are six methods you may find useful:

1. *The Thinking Game.* Write several problems and answers on the blackboard. Have the class study them for several minutes. Erase and write them again, arranging the combination in another form. Do not include answers. Children must write the answers.

2. *Fox and Geese.* The fox stands in the center of a circle. He calls on a goose by name and announces a combination of numbers. If the sum or difference is not given correctly, the goose is caught and joins the fox in the circle. Then another goose is called upon and another combination announced. The goose in the circle may escape by calling out the answer before the pupil can. If he does, the pupil comes to the center of the circle with the fox.

3. *Stepping Stones.* Draw a stream and stepping stones from one bank to the other on the blackboard. The stones should be drawn to allow several different routes across the stream. Write a combination of numbers on each stone.

   The children choose routes to cross the stream by answering combinations. If an error is made, the pupil falls into the stream. This technique can be used as a basis for a racing game.

4. *Pussy in the Corner.* Pupils are arranged in a circle. One student is selected to be "it." Each pupil is given a

number, but each number is given to two pupils. The pupil who is "it" announces a combination of numbers, such as seven and five. The two pupils who have the number 12 scamper to exchange places as quickly as possible. If the pupil who is "it" can reach a position before one of the others, the student he displaces becomes "it." If not, he announces another combination. The game can be used for subtraction drill as well.

5. *Winging Wild Geese.* Arrange nine digits on the blackboard in V formation. Let digits run in random order and change the order frequently. As a "bullet," use any number from two to nine. The object is to add, subtract, multiply, or divide the "bullet" and digits.

6. *The Guessing Game.* Announce, "I am thinking of two numbers, the sum of which makes   ." The children try to guess the combination. The one who guesses correctly takes a turn. The game can also be used for subtraction, division, and multiplication drill.

Chapter 9. A COMPENDIUM OF SCIENCE ACTIVITIES

SUMMARY OF TECHNIQUES

9

A COMPENDIUM OF
SCIENCE ACTIVITIES

The scope of the science curriculum in an elementary class-room should be determined in part by the basic personal and social needs of individuals and groups. Through science, children are assisted in recognizing and understanding significant facts and in using them intelligently.

Science is continuous, and work during elementary school years should be planned to develop functional understandings of the principles, attitudes, and phases of the scientific method. In defining the extent of each year's science program, the teacher should consider the scope of the entire curriculum, the work of preceding years, and the predictable interests, abilities, and needs of the children.

A major obstacle to proper scientific development is often the inability to evaluate the effectiveness of the curriculum. The following guidelines may assist you in determining the degree to which your class has grasped and is using scientific principles:

• Have the children acquired a knowledge of the fundamental processes of nature?

• Do they demonstrate ability to name and describe common natural phenomena in their immediate environment?

• Do the children show that they recognize the influence of natural forces upon their lives?

• Do they show increasing interests in the natural world and in the man-made world of science?

• Do they demonstrate a development of skills appropriate for interpreting scientific phenomena?

AN ANIMAL DICTIONARY

During a unit on animals in grades two to four, the class can make an animal dictionary using large story paper for pages and binder rings to keep pages together. Binder rings allow pages to be removed, shifted, and added.

Encourage children to bring pictures of animals to class. These can be cut out of magazines and newspapers. They also should be encouraged to draw pictures of animals.

Paste pictures and drawings on paper and place them in alphabetical order in the dictionary. The name of the animal should be written on the page.

Another idea that can be employed during a unit on animals is to have children construct insects from corrugated cardboard for parts of the body and from pipe cleaners for legs and antennae. Real or imaginary animals can also be fabricated from tin cans and construction paper.

CROSS DISCIPLINING

Lessons in science can often be introduced during classes in other subjects. For example, a lesson concerning how animals protect themselves can be introduced in gym by allowing the children to play a game in which one group is composed of "foxes" and another of "hunters." The objective of the "foxes" is to use their speed to escape from the "hunters."

When you start the science lesson, you can ask, "In gym, the foxes tried to protect themselves from the hunters. How did they do this?"

When the children answer, "by their speed" or "by running fast," you can state: "This is the way foxes protect themselves. All animals have ways to protect themselves from hunters, from other animals, and from danger. Let's see what these ways are."

Before class, cover a bulletin board with a sheet of flannel material. Prepare signs to denote ways in which animals protect themselves. A piece of sandpaper glued to the backs of signs will allow them to stick to the flannel. Examples of signs are those showing or denoting claws, teeth, speed, color, hoofs, and horns.

Also prepare pictures of animals that you have clipped from magazines and newspapers. Mount each on oaktag, and glue a piece of sandpaper to their backs. Stack these pictures in a pile near the bulletin board.

The idea of the lesson is to allow children to match the protective devices with the proper animal or animals. At the end of the lesson, the bulletin board is completed. Allow it to remain in place for several days to permit pupils to examine it.

To add emphasis to the lesson, you can bring a small animal, such as a chameleon, to class so children can see how it changes color according to surrounding conditions.

TEACHING THE CHARACTERISTICS OF AIR

Several experiments can be conducted to show the characteristics of air pressure during a unit dealing with weather in grades five and six. These are as follows:

1. To show that air occupies space, fill a bowl half full of water. Invert a glass tumbler and put it gently into the bowl. The air in the tumbler will force the water level to rise.

2. To show that air has pressure, suck water into a straw. Hold your thumb over the top of the straw. Water remains in the straw, because air pressure pushes up on the water from below but not down from above. Remove your thumb. Air rushes in from above and pushes

water out. Explain that at sea level air exerts a force of 15 pounds per square inch.

3. To further demonstrate that air has pressure, peel the shell from a hard-boiled egg. Ignite a small piece of paper and push it into a milk bottle. Lay the egg over the top. As the paper burns, it consumes the oxygen inside the bottle. The egg is drawn into the bottle, because a partial vacuum has been created. Air exerts a greater pressure on the egg from the outside of the bottle than from the inside.

ANOTHER AIR PRESSURE EXPERIMENT

Fill a gallon bottle with water, leaving space around the neck. Weight a cork with a large nail, so that it barely floats.

Place another cork into the neck of the bottle as a stopper. This compresses the air above the water which, in turn, presses down on the floating cork. The cork is forced down by air pressure and sinks to the bottom. Remove the stopper, and the cork bobs to the surface.

SCIENCE ACCORDING TO THE SEASONS

A number of leisure-time and seasonal interests provide occasion for science activities. These could include caring for classroom pets, planting, keeping an aquarium, visiting a zoo, collecting leaves, collecting seeds, collecting rocks and minerals, and feeding birds.

These activities are scientific. They develop understanding of and regard for cause and effect relationships, careful observation, accurate description, and impersonal appraisal.

In connection with activities that tend to be repeated year after year, you should acquaint yourself with what has been taught in preceding grades. Plan an instructional program which carries the learning to a higher level of maturity.

The chart in Figure 9-1 is offered to give an idea of the seasonal activities that can be developed.

Seasonal and Continuous Activities Common to All Elementary Levels

	AUTUMN	WINTER	SPRING AND SUMMER	CONTINUOUS
PEOPLE	Clothing Foods Fuel Fall games and harvest festivals	Clothing Heating Indoor life Household science	Clothing Cleaning Foods Activities	Clothing Foods Housing Health
PLANTS	Seed dispersal Leaf collection	Dormancy	Growth Budding Wild flowers	Indoor gardening Terraria
ANIMALS	Migration Storing food	Winter "clothing" Winter wildlife Bird feeding Hibernation	Return of birds Insects Pond life	Aquaria Pets Feathers Protection
WEATHER	Coolness Fog Frost	Storms Snow and ice	Warmth Rain Dew	Thermometer Air Water
ASTRONOMY	Shorter days Fall skies Harvest moon	Winter skies Aurora borealis	Longer days Spring skies Clouds	Star legends
ROCKS AND STONES	Minerals Fossils Stones		Soils	Collections

Figure 9-1.

PLOTTING THE BIRDS

One of the best ways to introduce a study of bird migration is to plot the route of several migratory birds This can be done by posting an outline map of North America, Mexico, and Central and South America on the bulletin board.

Accumulate information about migration. Data should include reasons for migration, routes followed, and distances traveled. Try to select birds which travel different routes. It is also a good idea to select a bird that migrates through the area in which you are located. If this is possible, have children keep a record of the dates on which the bird starts to migrate and the day it returns.

Stress that not all birds follow the same route in the Fall as they do in the Spring.

WHAT CAUSES DAY AND NIGHT

In discussing the causes of day and night, concepts you will wish to impart are: the earth rotates on its axis and makes a complete rotation every 24 hours; the earth rotates from west to east; the sun's rays shine on only half the earth at a time; we have day when our part of the earth faces the sun; we have night when our part of the earth faces away from the sun; the earth's rotation causes day and night. These points can be demonstrated through use of a globe, sticks, flashlight, and other materials.

Activities can include the following:

1. Shadows that move (created by means of shadow sticks) can demonstrate the movement of the earth. Using a compass, have the children determine east and west. Ask them in which direction shadows move (in the morning, shadows point west; at noon, they point north; in late afternoon, shadows point east).

2. Let one child hold a globe. Let two other pupils, holding appropriate east and west signs, stand on each side of the globe. The child holding the globe should be instructed to turn to east.

3. A globe can also be used to demonstrate the earth's rotation on its axis.

4. Darken the room and shine a flashlight on the globe. Regardless of where the light ray hits the globe, only half of it is lit. Ask such questions as, "Where on the globe is it night?"; "Where is it day?"; "How can day become night?"

To demonstrate to children that shadows indeed move, have them mark the position of a shadow cast on the floor by an object at various times during the day.

EXPLAINING THE SEASONS

When explaining the seasons to elementary grade pupils, concepts you may wish to emphasize are the following:

• While the earth is rotating, it revolves around the sun.

• The earth takes 365 days to make one trip around the sun.

• Long ago, people thought the sun moved around the earth.

• Like the earth, the sun also rotates on an axis, but the earth's axis and that of the sun do not point in the same direction.

• The earth's axis always points in the same direction as it moves around the sun.

• If a certain amount of heat is spread over a fairly large area, it will not be as hot as an equal amount concentrated on a smaller area.

• We have different seasons because the earth is tilted on its axis.

• We have summer when the northern half of the earth is tilted toward the sun.

• We have winter when the northern half of the earth is tilted away from the sun.

• Between winter and summer, we have autumn and spring.

• In the summer in our hemisphere, we have warm weather because days are longer and sunlight is more concentrated.

• In the winter in our hemisphere, we have cold days because the days are shorter and the sunlight is more spread out.

Activities that can be presented to demonstrate these concepts are as follows:

1. Demonstrate the earth's two motions (rotation and revolution) by placing a lamp (sun) in the center of a large circle. Let a student (earth) walk around the circle, spinning as he walks. Point out that if the child were really the earth, he would make 365 spins while making one trip around the sun.

2. If the concept concerning the earth's motions requires further clarification, use a ball with a long rubber string attached to it. Wind the string around the ball from right to left. Swing the ball slowly around the lamp (sun) to represent the earth's revolution. As the string unwinds from left to right, the earth's rotation will be represented. Both revolution and rotation will occur at the same time.

3. Use papier-mâché models, suspended from a board, to demonstrate the position of the earth and sun axes.

4. Use flannel board (and/or chart) to depict the position of the earth's axis, emphasizing that it always points in the same direction, as the earth moves around the sun.

5. To demonstrate the strength of heat while in the sunlight, hold a small reading glass over paper. Make a small circle. The paper will burn. Now, hold the glass to form a large circle. The paper will not burn. This demonstrates the concept that a certain amount of heat spread over a fairly large area is not as hot as an equal amount of heat concentrated in a small area.

6. Use a lamp light to represent the sun and a globe to represent the earth. Tilt the axis of the globe so the part of the earth where you are located is pointed toward the sun. Hold a piece of paper in which is punched a small square hole between sun and earth, causing a spot of light to fall on your area.

   Keeping the same distance between light, paper, and globe, tilt the axis so the place where you are located is away from the sun. Hold the paper, so a spot of light falls on this same area. Now, ask the question, "The same amount of light shows through the hole, but which spot is bigger?"

7. On the chart you used to depict the position of the earth's axis, point out the northern part of the earth tilting toward the sun for part of the year, while the southern part of the earth is pointing away from the sun. Show that at another time of the year the northern half of the earth is tilting away from the sun while the southern part points toward the sun.

8. Make and show a chart demonstrating the rays of the sun on the tilted earth. Place the names of the four seasons in their proper positions.

9. To emphasize the fact that we get more sunlight and daytime during the summer, discuss daylight activities which the children do in summer and winter, the use of electricity in the home, the time when street lights go on, and the like.

MAKING A GARDEN

An interesting and educational activity involves making a garden using eggshells. Have children bring eggshell halves and egg cartons to school. The eggshell halves must be intact.

Let them decorate the cartons with paint or cover them with colored paper. Place the eggshells in the cartons and fill the halves with soil. Plant seeds in each half and label it with the name of the child who is designated as its caretaker.

WORKING WITH THERMOMETERS

You can employ several activities in teaching thermometer concepts to students in grades two to four. Suppose, for example, you wish to demonstrate the principle that cold makes mercury descend while heat makes it rise. The following activities stress this concept:

1. Let the children observe what happens to mercury in a thermometer when it is placed in cold water or snow,

or is hung outside on a cold day. Let them see what happens when a thermometer is held near a radiator or steampipe, or is hung out the window in the sun's rays. Explain that there is only air above the mercury in the thermometer tube.

2. Demonstrate the basic principle of thermometers by filling a glass bottle with water and adding a drop of red ink. Place a one-hole stopper fitted with a glass tube into the bottle's neck. Mark the water level on the tube with a rubber band or piece of string. Place the bottle in a pan of hot water. Action of the water simulates thermometer action when the latter is heated.

3. Bring several different types of thermometers to class and discuss whether they all work in the same manner.

Another concept concerning thermometers is that at 32° on the Fahrenheit scale water will freeze, while at 212° on this scale water will boil. Have the children make temperature scales. A piece of cardboard will serve as the scale. Make holes near the top and bottom of the cardboard. Extend two strings between the holes, so they extend around the front and rear of the cardboard and are tied together in the rear. One string can be red; the other, white. Manipulating the strings from the rear will make the thermometer scale go up and down.

You can make a large model of this scale by using ribbons instead of string.

This activity permits the following learning opportunities:

• Gives practice in reading a thermometer.

• Gives practice in reading and writing numbers from below zero to above 212, depending upon the range of the scale.

• Gives practice in the use of fraction concepts for reading odd-numbered temperatures, such as 77°.

• Gives practice in subtracting to find differences in temperature readings.

• Allows the use of comparisons, such as higher and lower, and more and less.

Another thermometer concept is that different substances have different freezing points. You can demonstrate this on a cold day. Place different fluids (water, oil, alcohol, and glycerine, for example) into separate jars and place them outside the window. Position a thermometer near the jars, and allow children to observe results frequently.

You may wish to introduce the concept that mercury and most other substances expand as they get hotter, by introducing an experiment which demonstrates how heated air expands. Connect a balloon to a flask. When the flask is heated, the balloon inflates.

Still another concept is that a thermostat holds temperature at a steady reading. Tell the children that the temperature in the classroom is kept at a constant, comfortable level by the action of the thermostat in the room. Ask the school engineer to remove the cover from the room's thermostat and explain its operation to the class. Take them to the school's boiler room and show them the operation of boilers and ventilating system. You can explain that the same principles apply to the operation of furnaces and thermostats in their homes.

Another concept dealing with thermometers is that clinical thermometers record how hot the human body is. You can ask the school doctor or nurse to take the temperatures of several students. The children can determine normal human body temperature from these.

Finally, introduce the concept that if one is measuring the temperature of air, one must not touch or breathe on the thermometer bulb. Have the children note a thermometer reading. Then, have them breathe on the bulb and touch it. Have them again record the reading.

TREES AND LEAVES

Which concepts are you introducing to students in grades two and three during a unit on trees? The following concepts will serve as a guide in formulating your unit:

1. Trees are living things. They are plants. They need food, air, sun, and water to live and grow. The stems of trees are the trunk, limbs, and branches.

2. Stems transport food and water to the tree as a whole. Leaves make food for the tree. Roots gather food and

water from the soil. The number of roots beneath a tree approximates the number of branches on the tree. Seeds for new trees come from old trees. As a tree grows, the trunk gets larger and the branches get longer.

3. Different trees have different shapes and different-shaped leaves. Trees with needle-shaped leaves are evergreens. They keep their leaves year round. Trees with flat, wide leaves are broad-leaved trees. Most of these lose their leaves in the fall and get new leaves in the spring. The biggest tree of all is the Sequoia.

4. Trees give us shade, food, and wood. Roots of trees hold water in the ground to make the land around us beautiful.

5. In the spring, leaves are green. In late summer, leaves start to turn color. The red, yellow, and orange colors we see in the fall have really been on the leaves all the time. These colors were just covered with green. In the late summer, the green fades to uncover the bright colors beneath. The colors stay with us until the fall when the leaves drop off the trees.

6. A tree usually has leaves of one shape. There is, however, one tree which has four different shaped leaves on one branch. It is called the sassafras tree.

7. Trees are good friends to people, animals, and the land.

WATCHING THE WEATHER

One of the most interesting scientific activities for pupils in grades one to four is keeping a daily weather chart. Each child can record the times of sunrise and sunset, temperatures at certain periods of the day, wind direction at certain periods of the day, and weather conditions for the day.

Symbols can be introduced. You can employ official weather bureau symbols or devise your own. A master chart can also be prepared and hung on the bulletin board.

Figure 9-2 is a sample of a chart format you might use.

Science
Weather Chart

Name _____

Date	Sunrise	Sunset	Temp. 9 a.m.	Temp. 2 p.m.	Wind 2 p.m.	Weather

sunny   partly cloudy   cloudy   rain   sleet   snow   fog

Figure 9-2.

SETTING UP A TERRARIUM

In science, children should be trained to observe and think. "Why does this happen?" "How long does it take to happen?" "How do animals act under certain conditions?" "What was needed to get this plant to grow?"

Great emphasis can be placed on observation and thinking by establishing model scientfic communities in the classroom. In this way, children can observe plants and animals in their natural habitat. One of these communities is a terrarium. The following suggestions will help you in establishing this project.

Secure a clean terrarium or aquarium that has a sloping front and removable top. Cover its bottom with sand to a depth of about one inch. Mix a generous supply of coarse pepples into the sand. On top, add about one and a half inches of humus. Mix sphagnum or peat moss with the humus.

The sand and humus may be heaped in one of the four corners or at one end of the terrarium to obtain a terrracing effect. However, maintain appropriate depths for each.

There is no need to fertilize the terrarium soil.

The arrangement of plants to be included in the terrarium should approximate their natural conditions. For example, Marchantia should be given a certain amount of cover by surrounding plants.

Arrange plants for maximum individual display value. Thalloid and low-lying plants, such as Marchantia and Conocephalum, may be placed in the front of the terrarium. Lycopodium, Selaginella, Mosses, and Lichens should be placed next in line. Finally, tall plants such as Pitcher Plants, Venus Fly Trap and Fern should come next.

If terrarium plants are sufficiently anchored in an upright position, necessary rooting will be accomplished.

Keep the layer of humus moist. Be careful, however, that water does not percolate down into the sand to completely saturate it. This may lead to souring of the soil. If puddling is noted in any area, allow the terrarium to dry out before adding more water.

Chameleons, frogs, and turtles make good terrarium animals. They can be fed flies in warm weather and meal worms in cold weather. Do not allow food to decay in the terrarium. Remove surplus food. A few snails will act as scavengers.

Place a wire screen cover over the exposed surface to prevent animals from escaping. The cover will also serve as a means of ventilation to help reduce mold growth on plants.

Place the terrarium in a position so it benefits from light. It need not be in direct sunlight for more than two or three hours a day.

Minimize sudden changes in temperature. For example, do

not place the terrarium over or near a radiator. Coal and gas fumes may kill plants and animals. Keep the terrarium away from an open window where this might occur.

SETTING UP AN AQUARIUM

To establish a healthy aquarium, you must have the correct kinds of plants and animals in the proper ratio. Water must be clear, and light and temperature conditions must be ideal.

Trying to secure these balanced conditions often leads to problems. The following suggestions, then, may help you in this endeavor.

Secure a clean tank. Test for leakage by filling it with water and allowing it to stand overnight.

Place a layer of garden soil, at least one-half inch deep, in the tank. Cover with a layer of clean, washed sand to a depth of from one to two inches. Make the sand more shallow toward the front of the tank to allow sediment and waste material to collect for siphoning.

Add clean pond water, spring water, or aerated tap water slowly to the tank, pouring it onto a piece of clean paper or glass to keep sand from stirring. If chlorinated water must be used, boil it and then allow it to stand overnight before adding it to the tank. Before pouring this water into the tank, pour it back and forth from one receptacle to another for aeration.

Put plants into the tank first. Place rooted plants, such as Vallisneria and Sagittaria, toward the back corners of the tank in the deepest sand. Place roots well into the sand, but do not cover leaves.

Other plants, such as Elodea, Cabomba, Myriophyllum, and Ceratophyllum, may be placed toward the center and front of the tank. Plant these into the sand. If they begin to float free, anchor them into the sand with pebbles or small lead strips.

Lemna (duckweed), Azolla, Salvinia, and Riccia Fluitans are floating plants. Chara and Nitella may either float or be anchored basal and downward.

Use plants sparingly. Too few are better than too many. Overstocking the tank may cause all plants to die.

If water is not clear, wait until suspended matter has settled before adding animals. Use snails, mussels, tadpoles, and fish. Aquatic newts or small turtles can be introduced if a floating platform is provided. Avoid animals which are not compatible, and do not use too many. One inch of live fish to each gallon of water is a good rule. Goldfish are not recommended. They destroy vegetation.

Locate the aquarium in a well-lighted area where sunshine is available at some time during the day. In a northern latitude, a southern exposure during winter months is desirable. The same exposure during spring and summer, however, will require that you shade the tank because of excessive heat.

Allow light to strike the aquarium from above. Do not permit more than two hours of direct sunlight each day, especially during warm weather. A glass plate should be placed over the aquarium to prevent excessive water evaporation, to shield the tank against dust, and to keep fish from jumping out.

Exercise care to protect the aquarium from sudden temperature changes. Place the tank a short distance away from the window, but do not place it near a radiator. The ideal temperature is between 40° and 60° Fahrenheit. Do not allow water to freeze. A large tank of water has slower temperature fluctuations than a small tank.

Since a newly established aquarium lacks sufficient food for animal and plant life, place a small amount of boiled lettuce leaves in the water for snails and tadpoles. Use lettuce sparingly, and do not leave it in the water for more than a few hours. Decaying material will easily contaminate the water.

Feed fish small amount of tiny worms, Daphnia (water fleas), or prepared fish food.

If soil is used under the sand, plants will require little extra food. If plants do not develop a healthy green color, however, add a small amount of fully soluble plant food, but use it sparingly.

Remove dead matter promptly. Water that develops a cloudy appearance is usually the result of overstocking or an unfavorable plant-to-animal ratio. An abundance of algae on the glass may be formed by too much light and may require that you shade the tank with a green cloth. Scrape excess algae away with a razor blade.

Remember that the important factors in cultivation of a successful aquarium are light, temperature, oxygen, and nutrients. These factors can be impressed on your students. Frequent observation and a sustained interest in the project will best help students profit from the experience.

HOW THE SUN AFFECTS PLANT GROWTH

This is an exercise for the primary grades. Have children plant identical vegetable seeds in separate flower pots. Set one pot to receive maximum sunlight. Set the other in a dark corner, closet, or cupboard. Give each plant the same amount of moisture and other care. Have children compare the growth and development of young plants from time to time.

CLOCKING THE SUN

Students can plot the sun's position in the sky at various times during the day by means of a homemade sun dial. Use a smooth board about eight inches square for the dial face, and a ten pennyweight nail for the indicator (gnomon).

Drive the nail vertically into the board's center, leaving most of the shank protruding. Position the board outside the window on the south side of the building, if possible. Or, if desirable, place the board in an open area away from the school.

Have students note the position of the shadow cast by the indicator at 9 A.M. Mark the position on the dial face. Do the same at noon and again at 3 P.M.

Mark the 6 P.M. position opposite the noon position. The dial is now divided into quarters. On the next sunny day, mark in the hours.

TEACHING SCIENCE
BY OVERHEAD PROJECTION

Use of an overhead projector affords several opportunities to present scientific material in an interesting, absorbing manner.

For example, you can prepare and project pictures, graphs, and written material from scientific and other publications, including *Scientific American, Nature and Science, Science, Life, National Geographic, Newsweek,* and *Times.* You can do the same with clippings from old texts and workbooks, and with sketches that you draw.

To give you an idea of how projection can be employed in the elementary science class, the following ideas are offered:

1. Children in primary grades often have trouble understanding day and night concepts. Well-drawn transparencies showing the shadowed side of the earth in relation to the sun's position can help them understand that sun lights the solar system and, therefore, provides day; that rotation takes one side of the earth away from the sun and, therefore, produces night.

2. Plant science can be taught by means of the overhead projector. For instance, when teaching the corresponding growth of root and stem systems in germinating seeds, make sketches of: the seed, rootlet, sprouting shoot and growing root system, growing stem and foliage, and spreading root system.

   Reproduce each sketch on a separate sheet of transparent material. Color them if you wish. The seed can be colored yellow; the rootlet, brown; the growing root system, brown; the sprouting shoot, green; the spreading root system, brown; and the growing stem and foliage, green.

   The transparency showing the seed is the base transparency. All others are overlays. The base transparency stays in place on the projector during the demonstration. One by one, each overlay is placed on top of it. In making transparencies, therefore, each overlay has to be aligned perfectly with the base transparency.

   The base transparency is placed in a mounting frame. The three overlays are hinged to the frame in the proper sequence of germination (rootlet, sprouting shoot, growing stem), so they can be flipped, in turn, over the seed. This shows the full growth cycle of a plant.

3. In teaching the principles of a weather map to grades five and six, use a series of ten transparencies. Tape or clip a worksheet to the side of each for reference during the lecture.

The ten transparencies are made as follows:

    a. Reproduce a detailed weather map, which you can obtain from the weather bureau or newspaper. Use it as a basis for discussion of the importance of weather maps to industries such as airlines and steamships.

    b. Trace an outline map of the United States on to a sheet of plain white opaque paper and draw an airplane in its center. Draw an arrow pointing to the plane's tail.

    c. Make another map as in (*b*) above. Draw in an arrow to portray a head wind. The two sketches (*b*) and (*c*) are used to demonstrate to students that wind forces can accelerate or decelerate a plane above or below the speed set by the captain.

    d. Draw an outline map of the United States. Draw in three sweeping arrows coming from different directions to portray wind direction. Write numerals above each arrow to signify altitude of wind currents. Use this transparency to demonstrate that wind direction varies at different altitudes, and that a pilot must select the best altitude at which to fly to keep his plane from being hampered by the wind.

    e. Sketch four wind symbols on a sheet of white opaque paper to signify four different wind directions and velocities. Reproduce them on to a sheet of transparency material, so each is equidistant from the others. Run a strip of black plastic tape horizontally across the transparency and another vertically down its center. This divides the transparency into four parts. Cut out four cardboard rectangles to cover each of the four parts and tape them to the sides of the transparency. Using a grease pencil for sketching on the transparency, introduce each of the four symbols in turn, explaining how the wind arrow tells the direction and speed of the wind.

f. Prepare another transparency as in (e) above. This time reproduce each of the symbols on a different colored transparency material, such as red, blue, yellow, and green. Trim each and place them in a mounting frame, using the masking technique explained above. Use this transparency technique to demonstrate that letters and shading within a wind symbol's circle tell sky conditions. For example, R signifies rain, S means snow, a half-shaded circle means partly clouded, and a fully shaded symbol means complete overcast.

g. Another transparency can consist of a cartoon to depict how wind velocity appears to people on the ground. For example, it can show a house with smoke coming lazily out of a chimney and a tree standing upright. On top of the drawing, write in the wind symbol for a one to three mile an hour wind.

h. This transparency shows the same cartoon as in (g) above, except that smoke from the chimney and the tree are drawn to depict a gustier wind. The symbol for an eight to 12 mile an hour wind is drawn in.

i. Again, the transparency is the same as (g) above, except a very gusty wind is portrayed. The symbol for a 25 to 31 mile an hour wind is drawn in.

j. This is a quiz transparency. Make a map possessing correct symbols discussed in class. Before projecting it, pass weather maps to children and quiz them on symbols. When you project the transparency, children can determine if their answers are correct.

TRANSFORMING FLOWERS

An interesting experiment with flowers can be performed with sulphur and a glass tumbler to show how flowers react to sulphur fumes. Do not perform this experiment with pets in the room, and keep children at a safe distance from the flame.

Place one-half teaspoon of powdered sulphur on a nonflammable surface, such as an old saucer or metal lid. Light with a match. Turn a glass tumbler upside down over the burning sulphur, but allow sufficient air space to keep sulphur burning.

When the sulphur has just about burned itself out, pick up the tumbler and place it quickly over a flower. Fumes will remove the color from the flower, because sulphur fumes act as a bleaching agent.

Another experiment demonstrates how color can be added to a white flower. Place a small amount of commercial dye in water and put the stem of a white flower in the water for about one hour. The flower will assume the color of the dye.

KEEPING A SEED CHART

Students in the second and third grades can make a seed chart in studying earth science. Encourage them to collect seeds and mount them on a large piece of cardboard. The seeds can be placed in small cellophane bags of the type used by stamp collectors. Glue the bags to the chart and catalog them, as follows:

1. Seeds we eat (peanuts, corn, beans, peas).
2. Vegetable seeds (onions, carrots, lettuce, tomatoes).
3. Flower seeds (sweet pea, petunia, pansy).
4. Seeds for squirrels (nuts, acorns).
5. Seeds for birds (wheat, rye, oats).
6. Seeds that give us clothing (cotton, flax).

HOW A TREE CHANGES

Have children in grades three and four record the seasonal changes a tree undergoes. Let each child select a tree near school or home, give it a name, and draw a picture of it once a month.

In early September, the tree will have most of its summer foliage. Advise the children to watch for seeds, nuts, or acorns. By October, the leaves will have turned a bright color and some may have fallen to the ground. By November, the tree will probably be bare.

During the winter months, have the children cut a small twig from the tree to study its buds and leave scars. In spring, have children watch for budding and flowers.

Each child can keep his drawings in a folder to have a month-by-month presentation of a tree's cycle.

STUDYING SOIL

Have students in grades four and five collect specimens of soil, including loam, gravel, sand, clay, and humus. Stress that each is usually a mixture of two or more kinds of soil. For a soil to be considered sand, for instance, it must contain more than half sand. Also explain that loam is a soil mixture that contains humus and is considered one of the best soils for growing plants.

Have children test various soils for their ability to absorb and retain moisture. Place an equal amount of each specimen into a separate container of the same size. Add an equal amount of water to each to determine the absorption characteristics. Students will see that water disappears quickly in coarser soils (gravel and sand), and that very little moisture clings to them. On the other hand, finer soils (clay, humus, and loam) may give a flooded appearance.

Place the containers in the sun and do not add more water. At the end of a week, examine each to see what has happened. The class will determine that water in the bottom of a container holding gravel will probably have disappeared. Sandy soil will probably be dry. Clay may have caked and hardened. Loam will probably still be moist.

Plant seeds in each container and add the same amount of water to each at the same time. The way in which the seed germinates, and the rate of plant growth can tell a class much about the character of the soil.

WHY THINGS FLOAT AND SINK

This can be an interesting scientific experience for students in grades five and six. Ask penetrating questions, such as, "Why does a big ocean liner stay afloat while a small nail will sink?" Activities to employ are as follows:

1. Have students place different substances in water to find objects that float and sink. Some woods, for example, float high in water, others float low, and others sink. A rock that floats is pumice.

2. Let the children experience the force of buoyancy. Put a cork in a pan of water. Let several children press it down. Ask them whether they feel the object pressing upward against their hand. This demonstrates that objects which float have an upward force when held down.

3. Measure the force of buoyancy. Weigh a rock by tying it to the hook of a spring balance. Submerge the rock in water and weigh it. A smaller weight will be derived than when weighing the rock out of water. This indicates that water helps to hold the rock up.

4. Demonstrate the principle of submarines by placing a stopper in a small bottle and place it in water. The bottle floats. However, the same bottle when filled with water and fitted with a stopper sinks. Carefully adjust the amount of water in the bottle to allow it to float just below the surface. Explain that submarines have devices for adjusting the relative amounts of water and air, allowing them to float or sink as desired.

5. "How can both sand and sawdust be recovered from a mixture of the two?" Show how water is used to separate mixtures by putting a sand-sawdust combination in a pan of water. Sawdust floats; sand does not. The two separate.

6. Demonstrate that heavy material can be shaped to let it float. Have students shape pieces of metal so they will float. Try floating a smoothly cut tin can. A little sand or gravel in the bottom of the can will keep it floating upright.

LEARNING ABOUT FIRE

In discussing fire and its importance to man, certain basic concepts will want to be stressed to pupils in grades three and four. These are:

1. A supply of air is necessary for a fire.
2. Something to burn is necessary for a fire.
3. Some way of getting the fuel hot enough to burn is necessary for a fire.
4. Ashes of a material usually occupy less space than the material itself.
5. Unwanted fires may be prevented or put out by cutting off the air supply, by removing the fuel, and/or by keeping the burnable material cool.

Activities to support each of these concepts are the following:

1. To demonstrate that a supply of air is necessary for a fire, discuss reasons why leaves, paper, and other trash burn better in a wire basket raised off the ground than when piled on the ground. Also discuss the way in which logs are arranged in a fireplace. Stress why it is necessary to regulate drafts on stoves and furnaces.

2. To explain why there must be something to burn before you can have fire, collect samples of different materials. Show that some burn readily, while others do not. Include isinglass, celluloid, cotton cloth, paper, sawdust, corrugated board, wood, and coal.

3. To show that there has to be a way of getting the fuel hot enough to burn to make a fire, strike a match. Also try to make a fire with flint and steel. Use a discarded

steel file with a flint rock. You can make serviceable tinder by charring cotton cloth in an oven. Explain that automatic cigarette lighters utilize this principle.

4. You can demonstrate that ashes of a material usually occupy less space than the material itself by discussing the reasons why garbage is usually burned at the city dump. Have the school engineer tell children (or show them) that a bulk of material occupies so much space, while the same material when burned occupies less space.

5. To illustrate the principle that unwanted fires can be prevented or put out by cutting off air, by removing fuel or by keeping the combustible material cool, demonstrate how to smother fire. Show that a piece of burning cloth can be salvaged by rolling it in a piece of rug. Explain what should be done if clothing catches fire.

VINEGAR TRICKS

You can perform several experiments with household vinegar to stimulate the minds of pupils in grades two and three. Two of these are:

1. Put an egg into a bottle. Start the demonstration by explaining that a large egg can be put into a bottle which has a neck smaller than the egg. Use a milk bottle and a hard-boiled egg. Place the egg into a glass or ceramic pan of vinegar for several days. Do not remove the shell. When the shell has softened, squeeze the egg into the bottle. The shell will reharden and return to normal size. It will be impossible to remove the egg from the bottle.

2. Tie knots in bone. Bring several rib bones to school. Clean them and put into a glass or ceramic pan filled with vinegar for about a week. At the end of this time, the bones will be soft enough to tie into knots.

Chapter 10. USING IDEAS TO TEACH MUSIC

SUMMARY OF TECHNIQUES

10

USING IDEAS TO
TEACH MUSIC

Introduction of music to a child early in life will help him to understand and enjoy this important aspect of society in later years. Music also serves the elementary teacher by assisting her in teaching other disciplines.

This chapter and the one on art that follows, then, concern themselves with the teaching of art and music, and the employment of both as teaching devices.

OBJECTIVES OF A MUSICAL PROGRAM

Educators generally agree that a good musical program for elementary grade pupils should attempt to accomplish the following objectives·

1. To teach the child to appreciate music's contribution to the enrichment of his life.
2. To develop a liking for good music through group participation.
3. To aid in the development of the student's taste and discrimination.

173

4. To provide a permanent repertoire of folk and art music.
5. To develop in the child a sensitivity for the emotions of others as expressed through their art.
6. To assist the child in the acquisition of such skills and knowledge as are necessary for him to express himself.
7. To stimulate, discover, and develop musical talent in children.
8. To provide opportunity for the gifted child to make a contribution to the class.
9. To contribute to a richer life through a fusion of musical interests at school and home, and in the community.

MUSIC AND SOCIAL STUDIES

This idea, which can be introduced in grade four, permits two objectives: to foster rhythm in students and to acquaint them with the islands of the Caribbean.

Display a map of the Caribbean. Supply each student with a rhythm making instrument, such as two sticks or two hollow coconut shells. If no instruments are available, students can use their hands.

Pupils are instructed to point to an island on the map and pronounce its name. They are then asked, either individually or as a group, to sound out the rhythm which the island's name denotes with their instruments.

For example, suppose the island of Jamaica is selected. The rhythm that this name makes would be:

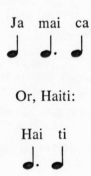

Ja   mai   ca

Or, Haiti:

Hai   ti

Or Puerto Rico:

Puer   to   Ri   co

Or Martinique:

Mar   ti   nique

This lesson is intended to stress that there is musical rhythm in many things, such as a country's name, the sound of a train's wheels on the tracks, and the sound of mother's high heels on a wood floor. It also serves as a prelude to the music of the Caribbean, which you may want to introduce in future lessons.

LEARNING ABOUT AMERICA THROUGH SONG

There are many songs about America which you can use in a social studies program. These include "East Side, West Side," "Bluebonnets of Texas," and "Old Paint." Each denotes characteristics of a region and emphasizes the grandeur of America.

"America the Beautiful" is a song taught in all schools. You can use a filmstrip, "America the Beautiful" (Bowmar), while teaching the song to add stress to the words.

INTERPRETING WORDS THROUGH SONG

You can often have children interpret words of a song by hand-and-arm motion. The technique serves to get pupils to interpret the mood of a song and to express the meanings of words.

For example, such words as *gracious, blessing, wondrous, kindness,* and *give thanks* in the song "Thanksgiving Canon" can be expressed as follows:

Phrase One: "For Thy gracious blessing"—have children place their hands across their chests and lower their heads.

Phrase Two: "For Thy wondrous words"—have children unfold their arms and place them straight down to their sides with eyes straight ahead.

Phrase Three: "For Thy loving kindness"—have children move their arms outward toward the center, with palms upward.

Phrase Four: "We give thanks, oh Lord"—have children raise their arms, palms inward, with their heads up and take one step forward.

MUSICAL PANTOMIME

Have children in grades two and three act out the words of a song. Use small groups while the class sings the song. Songs about animals are particularly suitable as, for example, "Three Blind Mice."

Have four, eight, or 12 pupils in front of the class arranged in a square formation, facing inward. As the class sings, the group acts out the words, as follows:

1. They take four steps toward the center.
2. They take four steps backward.
3. They take four steps to the right.
4. They take four steps to the left.
5. They take four steps to the center.
6. They take four steps back.
7. They take four steps around in place, with their hands shading their eyes.
8. They stamp their feet four times in place.

CLASS FIFE AND DRUM CORPS

Your class can have its own fife and drum corps by making instruments. Fifes are made from straight hollow reeds, such as pumpkin vines or bamboo poles. An ideal length is 14¼ inches. One end of the pole should be opened and the other end closed. If a pole has both ends open, close one end with beeswax or modeling clay.

To make the instrument's mouth hole, measure down two

inches from the closed end and cut an oval slit that is one-half inch long and three-eighths of an inch across. Measure down two inches from the open end of the rod, and drill or cut six holes along the length. Make holes one inch apart and slightly less than three-eighths of an inch in diameter.

Tunes are played by blowing into the mouth hole and covering holes with the correct finger combination. The player does not blow directly into the mouth hole, but across it on an angle.

Learning to play a fife may be difficult. Those who find it so should close part of the mouth hole with transparent tape.

Make drums from strong, round containers that have both ends removed. Ideal containers are about ten inches in diameter and 14 inches deep. They include small nail kegs, casein glue kegs, and large fruit juice cans. Children will also need strong string or leather thongs, a stout needle with a large eye, and two strong sticks to serve as drumsticks.

Cut two circles of chamois that are large enough to cover the ends of the container. Allow a generous overlap. Wet the chamois and stretch it tightly across the container openings. Lace the material together with string or leather thongs so they crisscross.

To make drumsticks, pad the ends of the sticks heavily with wadded cloth. Tie cloth to the sticks.

TUNES BY GLASSES

A set of 7 glass tumblers or glass bowls can be tuned to a musical scale by filling them with graduated amounts of water. Test the note that each glass makes on a piano or with a pitch pipe. Then label each with the letter designating the note or, if you prefer, with the note itself.

To make a hammer for striking the glass, wind strips of cloth around the end of a small stick and sew the cloth together. The class can play simple tunes with this self-made instrument.

H-U-M-M-M

The game is called "Who Is Humming?" A student is selected to be "it" and leaves the room. A hummer is selected. All pupils, including the hummer, rest their heads on their desks. When the student who is "it" returns to the room, the hummer begins to hum a tune and the student who is "it" tries to locate the hummer. The hummer can stop humming as he approaches. The student who is "it" is given a reasonable time in which to locate the hummer.

MUSIC IN THE ELEMENTARY SCHOOL

This section is a discussion of a musical project book compiled by an elementary school teacher. It has assisted her greatly in the teaching of music, and perhaps it can do the same for you.

The project book is divided into 15 chapters, which have the following titles:

Chapter 1. Songs About Our Country
Chapter 2. Songs from Other Lands
Chapter 3. Songs About Animals
Chapter 4. Songs to Sing on Holidays
Chapter 5. Songs About the Weather and Seasons
Chapter 6. Songs About Transportation
Chapter 7. Songs Without Words
Chapter 8. Songs That Ask Questions
Chapter 9. Songs About Sounds
Chapter 10. Songs of Make Believe
Chapter 11. Songs for Friendship and Brotherhood
Chapter 12. Songs About Space
Chapter 13. Songs Just for Fun
Chapter 14. Personal Recordings for Classroom Use
Chapter 15. Related Pictures

As you can see, the book serves as an excellent guide that can be referred to during the term. To make your book an effective teaching aid, it is suggested that the titles of specific songs you select be placed in envelopes which are pasted to pages of related chapters. As you uncover new ideas, they can be written on index cards and included. Related pictures and poems that can be used in conjunction with songs can also be added as they become available. Material for the reference book is obtained from song books, magazines, and other sources.

The following is a chapter breakdown with suggestions:

Chapter 1. *Songs About Our Country*. The songs you can paste into the book under this chapter heading are the following:

 a. "America the Beautiful"
 b. "Battle Hymn of the Republic"
 c. "Make America Proud of You"
 d. "Columbia, the Gem of the Ocean"
 e. "The Marine's Hymn"
 f. "The State Song" (*your* state)
 g. "Song of the Cactus Region"
 h. "East Side, West Side"
 i. "Shenandoah"
 j. "Upward Trail"
 k. "Dr. Ironhead"
 l. "There's a Little Wheel A-Turning"
 m. "I'm an Indian"
 n. "Bluebonnets of Texas"
 o. "Covered Wagon Song"
 p. "Night Herding Song"
 q. "The Cowboy's Sweet Bye and Bye"
 r. "Old Paint"
 s. "The Old Chisholm Trail"
 t. "Yankee Doodle"
 u. "Navajo Happy Song"
 v. "Song of the Eskimo"
 w. "The Indian Boy"
 x. "Never Be Afraid of Anything"

Chapter 2. *Songs From Other Lands*. The songs pasted into the project book under this chapter include:

 a. "Anna Maria, Wake Up!" (Brazilian)
 b. "San Sereni" (Spanish)
 c. "Celito Lindo" (Mexican)
 d. "The Ash Grove" (Welsh)
 e. "I Know Where I'm Going" (Irish)
 f. "Loch Lomond" (Scotch)
 g. "High in the Alps" (Swiss)

    h. "Vesper Round" (Russian)
    i. "One, Two, Three" (German)
    j. "The Seven Jump" (Dutch)
    k. "Shalom Chaverim" (Israeli)
    l. "Lotte Walked" (Danish)
    m. "Bell Yodel" (Austrian)
    n. "Waling at Night" (Czech)
    o. "Kee-Chee" (African)
    p. "Haru No Hi Urara" (Japanese)
    q. "Wung Fu" (Chinese)
    r. "Peter and Paul" (Hungarian)

Here are some suggestions for teaching rhythm and relating the song to the country. (1) Use maps to show students the location of the country where the song originated. (2) Clap the names of the countries and also write the names on the blackboard.

Integrate social studies into this area of the program. Many of the countries where the songs originated can be shown to the students on film strips. Also, several students can be asked to dress in the costumes of the country, and dances of the country can be learned with the songs. This is particularly applicable to an assembly program.

Chapter 3. *Songs About Animals.* Songs included in this chapter are:

    a. "Smokey the Bear"
    b. "The Bird Song"
    c. "The Donkey"
    d. "Old MacDonald"
    e. "The Circus"
    f. "The Kangaroo"
    g. "Peter Penguin"
    h. "Mr. Penguin"
    i. "Little Peter Rabbit"
    j. "Old MacDonald's Beehive"
    k. "Mr. Rooster"
    l. "Sweetly Sings the Donkey"

    m. "The Crocodile Song"
    n. "At the Zoo"
    o. "Three Blind Mice"
    p. "The Organ Man"
    q. "Over in the Meadow"

In integrating music with the language arts program, poems relating to animals can be introduced. One of these by Rowena Bastin Bennett is applicable during introduction of "The Circus":

> There were elephants blue,
> And shaggy white bears,
> And dozens and dozens of prancing grey mares
> With their beautiful heads held high.
>
> There were small curly dogs,
> And camels with humps,
> And a wrinkled rhinoceros, all over bumps;
> With a horn as big as your fist.

Chapter 4. *Songs to Sing on Holidays.* These include:

On Halloween:

    a. "I Saw Mr. Pumpkin"
    b. "Halloween Night"
    c. "Ooh-Ooh"
    d. "Witch Hunt"
    e. "Five Little Pumpkins"

On Flag Day:

"How Betsy Made the Flag"

On Thanksgiving:

    a. "Grace"
    b. "Turkey Times Mambo"
    c. "Thanksgiving Canon"
    d. "Pilgrim Children"
    e. "Come Ye Thankful People"

On Lincoln's Birthday:

"Honest Brave and True"

On Christmas:

a. "Joy to the World"
b. "Christmas Bells"
c. "O Little Town of Bethlehem"
d. "Jingle Bells"
e. "Santa's Coming"
f. "Christmas Comes Round"
g. "Santa's Workshop"
h. "Silent Night"
i. "Parade of the Wooden Soldiers"

On Chanukah:

a. "Chanukah"
b. "O Chanukah, O Chanukah"

Arts and crafts can be used with some of these songs. For example, at Halloween, have the class make finger pumpkins and act out the words of the song, "Five Little Pumpkins."

Chapter 5. *Songs About the Weather and Seasons.* Included in this chapter are the following:

a. "Summer Rhythm Round"
b. "Such a Bright Day"
c. "Spring's Coming, Spring's Coming"
d. "Like a Leaf"
e. "Winter Fun"
f. "Song of the March Wind"
g. "March Is an Actor"
h. "Spit, Spat, Spatter"

Poetry as a form of the language arts can be included with the music program in this area. When the song "Such a Bright Day" is introduced; for instance, the poem by Robert Louis Stevenson can be introduced:

"I woke before the morning, I was happy all the day. I never said an ugly word, but smiled and stuck to play."

In addition, many songs lend themselves to related music which you can play for the class. For example, the "Valse Gracieuse" by Dvořák can be played in connection with "Like a Leaf." Two parts of the music by Dvořák concern themselves with the gentle breeze and the noisy wind.

Chapter 6. *Songs About Transportation.* Songs you can use here are the following:

    a. "Bicycle Built for Two"
    b. "The Railroad Train"
    c. "Puffer Billies"
    d. "The Runaway Train"
    e. "Train Song"
    f. "I've Been Working on the Railroad"
    g. "She'll Be Comin' Round the Mountain"
    h. "Galloping Horse"
    i. "Where Go the Boats"
    j. "John the Boatman"
    k. "Yankee Clipper"
    l. "Tractor, Tractor"
    m. "The Bus"
    n. "Horsey, Horsey"

An opportunity to develop rhythm in children presents itself in many songs. For example, two hollowed-out coconut shells when clapped on wood resemble a horse's hoofs. This can be used rhythmically when the song "Horsey, Horsey" is introduced.

Many times, boys are reluctant to sing. By emphasizing that certain songs are he-man songs, you may get them to participate. Examples are "John the Boatman" and "Blow the Man Down."

Chapter 7. *Songs Without Words.* These include the following:

    a. "The Band on Parade"
    b. "The Indians Are Coming"
    c. "Marching Here and There"
    d. "Sambelele"
    e. "The Wild Horseman"
    f. "Dance of the Clowns"
    g. "Spring, Beautiful Spring"
    h. "Gique"

These songs, and others like them, may be used for rhythmic and interpretive experiences. They can be used in conjunction with language arts and social studies by permitting children to make up lyrics.

Chapter 8. *Songs That Ask Questions.* These include:

    a. "Would You Like to Know?"
    b. "Riddle Song"
    c. "Tell Me Why?"
    d. "Our Helpers"

These songs can be used in the language arts program. For instance, have children sing a song several times. Ask them to jot down words in a notebook that will help them remember the words of the song. This exercise gives them practice in taking notes.

Chapter 9. *Songs About Sounds.* Included are the following:

    a. "The Clock"
    b. "The Instruments"
    c. "Ring, Ring"
    d. "Telephone"
    e. "Orchestra Round"
    f. "Music in the Air"

Integrated activities can include the use of tone blocks. Call upon 12 children and let each take a block. Have the class listen for the lowest through the highest tone and arrange the 12 children in the correct order. This exercise helps develop the ear.

Chapter 10. *Songs of Make Believe.* Included here are the following:

    a. "Ring-a-Ring O' Fairies"
    b. "Come Follow Me"

Chapter 11. *Songs for Friendship and Brotherhood.* Included under this chapter are:

    a. "It Could Be a Wonderful World"
    b. "A Smile Is Quite a Funny Thing"

  c. "Hello! Hello!"
  d. "I Love That Word Hello"
  e. "You're a Friend of Mine"
  f. "Friend O Friend"
  g. "Mary Wore a Red Dress"
  h. "Dr. Sniffleswiper"

Chapter 12. *Songs About Space.* These can be integrated into the science program:

  a. "Beep Beep"
  b. "What Is the Milky Way"
  c. "Why Go Up There"

Chapter 13. *Songs Just for Fun.* Included in this chapter are the following:

  a. "One Finger, One Thumb"
  b. "There Were Three Jolly Fishermen"
  c. "Swinging Along"
  d. "The Grand Old Duke of York"
  e. "Little Boy Sambo Cha-Cha"
  f. "Hey Diddle Dum"
  g. "Let the Ball Roll"
  h. "Rig a Jig Jig"
  i. "Skipping Is Fun"
  j. "Never Be a Litterbug"
  k. "Prayer from Hansel and Gretel"
  l. "If You're Happy"
  m. "Head and Shoulders, Knees and Toes"
  n. "Hammer Song"
  o. "Dental Dialogue"

  The final two chapters of the project book, *Personal Recordings for Classroom Use* and *Related Pictures,* are addenda that you can prepare from personal belongings. The recordings can be played for children or be used in conjunction with lessons. Pictures, if used, should relate to the song that you introduce to the class.

Chapter 11. ARTS AND CRAFTS
AS CONTINUOUS STUDIES

SUMMARY OF TECHNIQUES

11

ARTS AND CRAFTS
AS CONTINUOUS STUDIES

Fostering an appreciation of art in children depends primarily upon your ability to develop a program which has reasonable flexibility in standards to meet the needs, abilities, and interests of pupils.

In most cases, art appreciation and graphic expression can be integrated into other areas of study. However, you may also find it desirable, especially in higher grades, to set aside time for teaching principles and basics. Another way to foster an appreciation for art is by displaying famous paintings. Often, paintings are available that can be used to emphasize units under discussion in science, social studies, and language arts.

What should be the objectives of an art program on the elementary level? Most agree, that they are the following:

1. Developing an appreciation of beauty in all things.
2. Stimulating the desire to create.
3. Affording many opportunities for experimentation, exploration, and manipulation of various materials.
4. Providing an understanding of art principles—order,

simplicity, balance, emphasis, repetition, and rhythm.
5. Providing knowledge of the correct use of art elements —tone, form, color, and texture.
6. Developing desirable habits, attitudes, and standards of taste.
7. Building a graphic arts vocabulary.
8. Relating art concepts to the school, home, and community.
9. Affording a recreational recourse and a foundation for art needs in later life.

ART AND THE ALPHABET

A class alphabet book in the primary grades combines language arts and art. A book 12 inches by 18 inches provides a neat presentation. Use regular art paper or butcher paper for pages. Make covers from oaktag.

The purpose of the book is to illustratively portray letters. Children can find pictures of objects in magazines. They should be encouraged to draw pictures. Several illustrations can be inserted for each letter.

The pages are organized by writing across the top of a page a letter and an object whose name begins with the letter, such as "A Is for Airplane," "B Is for Boy," and "C Is for Chair." The picture or drawing of the object occupies the remainder of the page.

ANIMAL MAKING

As part of a unit on animals, allow children to make their own animal stand-ups. Use wood from crates that you can obtain at a supermarket.

The pupils draw animals on colored paper. Two sheets of the colored paper are placed together, so that when the animal is cut out there will be duplicate figures.

Use one of the cut-outs as a pattern. It is placed on a piece of wood, and a silhouette is made. Cut out the silhouette with a small coping saw.

The colored paper cut-outs are then glued to the silhouette, one to each side, and the work is coated with shellac.

This idea can be used in several ways. For example, if a unit is concerned with the farm, domestic animals can be made. If you are presenting a unit on Africa, wild animals can be made.

SPATTER PAINTING

Spatter painting can be used in the classroom for decorating such things as greeting cards, for illustrating classroom projects, and for designing. It is done by laying a stencil on paper or cloth and spattering exposed parts with paint to produce a design.

To make a stencil, prepare the desired design on paper and transfer it by means of carbon paper to cardboard. Cut away the superfluous cardboard to make the design.

Prepare a stencil screen by fabricating a wooden frame about one foot square. Tack regular window screening across it.

Place the stencil on the material you wish to decorate and place the stencil screen atop it. Prop the arrangement up so the two components are about three-quarters of an inch above the surface to be decorated. Use a stiff bristle brush, such as an old toothbrush, and paint across the screen, pushing paint through.

SOAP CARVING

Don't overlook soap carving as an effective means of presenting art. Patterns are drawn on paper and transferred to soap by means of carbon paper. The figure is carved out with a penknife or small paring knife. Rough edges are smoothed with a damp cloth. You can add finishing colored touches with paint, or a mixture of colored sealing wax and denatured alcohol.

INTRODUCING PICTURE STUDIES

Picture studies in the elementary classroom should be made an integral part of a broad art appreciation program. For instance, good pictures can be used in connection with social studies, literature, science, and other subjects. Landscapes may be shown before a class is asked to paint or draw landscapes.

Good reproductions are valuable when discussing art techniques. For example, the paintings of Winslow Homer, John Marin, Van Gogh, and Cézanne are excellent examples of oil and water color techniques.

When discussing a picture, you can ask many thought-provoking questions, such as:

1. How does the artist show distance?
2. What does he do to make objects appear near and far?
3. How does he show a stormy day?
4. How does he draw our attention to the important thing he wants to convey?
5. Are all clouds of the same shape and size?

If pictures are discussed intelligently, the pupil will develop an understanding of the artist's problems and acquire a workable art vocabulary.

It is often desirable to display good examples of similar paintings so that contrast and treatment can be discussed. For example, famous paintings of weather can be shown. It is also interesting to compare several paintings of the same artist. Children will become better acquainted with his technique and learn to identify his work.

It is not possible to prescribe a definite set of pictures for each grade. It is better for each teacher to know and have available a list of sources from which to procure prints, slides, or films best suited to the interest and needs of her class.

You should be familiar with the works of modern as well as classical painters. The works of contemporary artists often hold greater appeal for children. Good prints are available at local artist supply stores and companies, and current magazines often publish good reproductions. In addition, most art museums have shops in which reproductions can be purchased.

The following are examples of the types of pictures you might want to present to your class:

Animals:
"Red Horses" by Franz Marc
Pictures by Henri Rousseau

Children:

"Lady Jean" by George Bellows
"Blue Boy" by Gainsborough
"Portrait of Vincente Osorio" by Goya
"The Graham Children" by Hogarth
"Prince Edward Tudor" by Holbein
"The Sackville Children" by Hoppner
"Little Margot Berard" by Renoir
"Boy with Rabbit" by Reynolds
"Miss Bowles" by Reynolds
"Torn Hat" by Sully

Flowers:

"Les Iris" by Van Gogh

Fruits.

Variety of still life studies by Cézanne

Landscapes:

"Mt. Ste. Victoire" by Cézanne
"The Blue Oak" by Derain
"Landscape with Road and Sportsmen" by Hobbema
"Tornado, Bahamas" by Winslow Hon.er
"Autumn Oaks" by George Inness
"The Lark" by Van Gogh
"Fishing in Spring" by Van Gogh
"Landscape with Kitchen Garden" by Van Gogh
"Tropical Scenes" by Henri Rousseau
"Arbor Day" by Grant Wood

Madonnas:

Madonnas of Botticelli
Madonnas of Raphael
"Virgin and Child" by Van Eyck

Mothers and others with children:

"Mother and Child" by Mary Cassatt
"The Storeroom" by DeHooch
"Marie Antoinette and Her Children" by Le Brun
"The Knitting Lesson" by Millet
"Mussel Gatherers" by Renoir

Religious pictures:

"St. Francis Preaching to the Birds" by Giotto

Workers:

"Men Are Square" by Benneker

"Going to Work" by Van Gogh

"The Milkmaid" by Vermeer

THE VALUE OF MUSEUM VISITS

Art appreciation is one result of having a class visit an art museum. Children enjoy viewing original works. However, they should be given some background before the visit to better understand what they will see. For example, one trip may be made to view landscapes. On other trips, the class can study composition, color, crafts, or portrait paintings.

GETTING NON-DRAWERS TO DO ARTWORK

Some children believe they can't draw. When the problem arises, try this technique to encourage the child.

Have him fold a piece of drawing paper into four squares. Drop a piece of yarn or string about 15 or 20 inches long into one of the squares. Have the child then draw the pattern the string makes. Have him copy the same pattern in all the squares. The child will be surprised to see the artistic design he has made and may be encouraged to do more.

BLINDFOLD DRAWING

Rainy day recess periods can be occupied by having students paint blindfolded. Select one student from the group who will not paint. He is director of the activity.

Have the students put on blindfolds at the blackboard. Blindfolds can be made of sheets of butcher paper which are fastened with paper clips.

The director now instructs the class in what to do. He uses the step-by-step method. For instance, he may direct the students to draw a dog.

"Draw the dog's body," he may instruct. "Now, his right eye and his left eye. Now his tail. Draw his front feet. Now his back feet. Now sign your name to the drawing."

The students remove their blindfolds and return to their seats to survey their efforts.

USING THE OVERHEAD PROJECTOR
TO TEACH ART

The overhead projector is a useful device for teaching art. For instance, it can be used to demonstrate lines, shapes, and lettering. Using felt markers for coloring on projection material allows you to have colorful programs. Color is easily erased with lighter fluid. Grease base crayons can also be used.

The overlay method is an excellent technique for teaching art. For instance, it can be used to show simple sketches for portrayal of good and bad design. Poor detail which ruins design balance can be drawn on overlay and introduced for discussion. You can also project overlapped tissue paper to show how colors are mixed.

Many teachers compile reproductions of famous paintings from magazines such as *Time* and *Life*. These can be reproduced in full color by means of the color-lift film process.

The following is one example of how overhead projection can be used in teaching art. It demonstrates the basic principles of design and can be used in grades five and six.

1. A checkerboard pattern is made in black and white using direct-reading-image positive transparency material. This forms the basic transparency.

2. A checkerboard pattern is then made to serve as over lay one. This is done by again reproducing the checkerboard pattern. This time, however, every second square is blackened. This demonstrates a formal design.

3. Overlay two is made by reproducing the checkerboard pattern on another sheet of transparency material. This time only one square is blackened. When this overlay is placed on top of the other two transparencies, it

demonstrates how the eye is attracted to the center of interest.

4. A third overlay is made in the same way, but this time two squares are colored different colors. This demonstrates how one color stands out above another to make a shape appear larger.

TEACHING CRAFTS BY PROJECTION

The overhead projector can be used to teach crafts. For example, suppose you want the children to make clay models, and want to show them how to work with clay.

As you know, it is difficult to hold the clay up and show manipulation in midair. Only children close to you are able to see clearly.

These difficulties are overcome by placing the clay on the stage of the overhead projector. The model outline is projected. All children can see what you are doing and can follow your action with their own models.

USING PROJECTION TO TEACH DRAWING

In grades five and six, use the overhead projector to instruct students in how to sketch portraits and figures. Suppose, for instance, you are lecturing on how to draw a head. Place a sheet of clear transparent film on the projector stage. Use a grease pencil and begin to draw. As you do, relate your lecture to the drawing. Students can follow easily, because they see as well as hear your instruction.

SPONGE PAINTING

Children in grades two and three enjoy using a wet sponge to paint on the blackboard. The technique helps to develop their rhythm and coordination.

After they sponge paint for a while, have them return to their desks and do the same thing on drawing paper. Let them use calcimine or poster paints and a small sponge.

CLASSROOM ART COLLECTION

Compilation of an art collection fosters appreciation for art. Pupils should be encouraged to collect works that have artistic merit. These can be obtained from magazines or by purchasing reproductions at art museums and art stores. Allow students who have talent to draw or paint pictures as their contribution to the classroom collection. Pictures can be placed in a large scrapbook or in folders.

MAKING PORTRAITS

Students in grades three to five will enjoy making silhouette portraits of classmates. Allow each student to pose. Place him between a sunny window and a smooth wall. Hang a sheet of light colored paper on the wall, so his shadow falls on the paper. Experiment until the silhouette is the desired size by moving the pupil closer or farther away from the wall. The outline of the silhouette is then sketched directly on to the paper. After it has been drawn, the silhouette is cut out and mounted on dark paper.

After silhouettes of all class members are made, arrange them into a border around the room for display. Visiting parents can see if they can pick out the silhouette of their child.

EXCHANGING BIRTHDAY CARDS

Encourage pupils to design birthday and other greeting cards for one another. Cards can be made to any size. An appropriate design or border can be selected. For example, peach blossoms can be selected for April, a snowman for January, colored leaves for October, and Santa Claus for December.

BLUEPRINT PICTURES

You can use this technique for decoration of greeting cards or as an art activity. Pupils will use blueprint paper, which can be purchased in an office supply store.

Have students select a flat flower, such as a pansy, or a leaf. Lay the object on a sheet of blueprint paper and hold it in place with a glass tumbler.

Place the setup in strong sunlight for about a minute to expose the blueprint paper. Take it back inside and apply a fixative of potassium bichromate with a sponge. Allow to dry, and cut out for mounting.

Blueprint pictures are excellent to use for decorating scrapbooks, greeting cards, stationery, and friezes. You can also use them for making displays for courses of study. For instance, blueprint pictures of flowers and leaves make good displays for a science exhibit.

LINOLEUM BLOCK PRINTING

Another method to use for decorating and display is block printing. Cut a piece of unembossed linoleum to fit a smooth rectangular or square block of wood. Blocks from one to eight inches are most suitable. Glue the bottom side of the linoleum to the wood block.

Make the desired design on paper and cut it out in silhouette fashion. Paste this on the linoleum. The cut-out serves as a guide to cut the block.

Use a penknife or block-printing cutting tool. Cut away the unnecessary parts of the block to a depth of about one-sixteenth of an inch. Now, apply oil paint or special block printing paint to the raised area. All supplies can be purchased in art supply stores.

Lay the material on paper upon a flat surface and place the block print face down on it. Press with a block print roller or an ordinary kitchen rolling pin. Remove the block and allow the material to dry.

Cloth, paper, and cardboard lend themselves to printing from linoleum block.